Pasta & Noodles

Above: Beef Ravioli with Hot Salami (page 92); Below: Chilli Satay Noodles (page 30)

Pasta & Noodles

Written & Compiled by
Jo Anne Calabria

Photography
Ray Joyce

Illustrations
Barbara Rodanska

CLB
Colour Library Books

The Pleasure of Pasta and Noodles

THE TASTE, TEXTURE and pure simplicity of pasta and noodles continue to delight and stimulate diners palates from all over the world. Derived essentially from a flour and egg or flour and water mixture, both pasta and noodles seem to transform even the most basic ingredients into simply delicious dishes.

In *Pasta and Noodles* we bring you the very best dishes, teaming pasta and noodles with seasonal vegetables and herbs, succulent seafood and rich meat, poultry and game. Discover classical dishes, family favourites and new innovative recipes, hearty soups, salads and main course dishes.

A great variety of pasta and noodles are available to purchase or make. Pasta comes in a diverse range of shapes and sizes, the names given to each type differ from region to region. The smallest difference in width or thickness may give pasta yet another name — to add to the confusion the same pasta shape may have a different name with each manufacturer. Noodle shapes do not vary as much as pasta, they may be thick or thin, flat or rounded but they will always be long.

In this book, we show you the great variety of dried and fresh pasta and noodles available, we give you a step-by-step guide to making your own pasta at home and the techniques for flavouring, rolling and shaping pasta. We make filling and shaping wonton noodles easy and give you the know-how to make perfect noodle baskets.

There's a wealth of information to help you cook perfect pasta and noodles every time. We discuss the different sauces that are ideally suited to the various pasta shapes and sizes and we look at the special ingredients used to enhance the many Asian inspired noodle dishes. Most importantly, we present you with a special collection of recipes, hints, tips and exciting ideas that work well, we give suggestions for interchanging the particular types of pasta shapes and noodles.

The joys of cooking pasta and noodles are immeasurable, with minimum effort they create maximum effect. We invite you to experience the pleasure of cooking and of course eating pasta and noodles.

JO ANNE CALABRIA

CONTENTS

FOR YOUR CONVENIENCE WE HAVE USED THE FOLLOWING COOKERY RATINGS TO GRADE EACH RECIPE

COOKERY RATING:

easy   a little care needed   for confident cooks

Pasta with Seasonal Vegetables

HERE WE GIVE YOU the very best of pasta teamed with ripe red tomatoes, fresh seasonal vegetables and the finest herbs. Freshly cooked pasta can be simply dressed with olive oil, freshly ground pepper and any lightly cooked fresh vegetables or beans. In this chapter we present hearty soups and main dishes including many Italian classics and family favourites.

Indulge your need for some comfort food with a bowl of Risoni and Mushroom Broth or Chilli Pappardelle with Cream Sauce. Turn your hand to Spinach and Pine Nut Ravioli with Buttered Mushrooms or a quick and easy Spiral Pasta Salad with Tomatoes, Olives and Feta, the choice is yours.

Clockwise from left: Spinach and Pine Nut Ravioli with Buttered Mushrooms, Tagliatelle with Dried Tomatoes and Snow Peas (page 10), Penne with Piquant Tomato Sauce (page 11)

Pea and Pasta Soup

A filling and nutritious Italian inspired soup. Traditionally chick peas would be used for this recipe, but being a dried pea they require long soaking and cooking before they are edible. Garbanzos are the canned equivalent and an excellent replacement in this recipe with no sacrifice of flavour or texture.

PREPARATION TIME: *12 minutes*
COOKING TIME: *15 minutes*
SERVES 4–6

¼ *cup olive oil*
2 cloves garlic, crushed
4 rashes bacon, rind removed and chopped
¼ *cup chopped parsley*
1 × 375 g can garbanzos
6 cups chicken stock
1 cup canned tomatoes, chopped
2 cups small shell pasta
freshly ground black pepper
extra ¼ *cup chopped parsley, for garnish*

1 Place oil in a large pan, add garlic and bacon cook for 4–5 minutes. Add parsley cook 1 minute longer.
2 Add garbanzos stock and tomatoes, bring to the boil, reduce heat and simmer uncovered for 5 minutes.
3 Purée half of the garbanzos mixture then return to the remaining mixture in the pan. Bring to the boil, add the pasta and cook until the pasta is just tender.
4 Place into serving dish or individual bowls, sprinkle with parsley. Serve.

White Bean and Pasta Soup

A thick vegetable based soup flavoured by the addition of ham hock. Try using small macaroni in place of spaghetti.

PREPARATION TIME: *10 minutes plus overnight soaking*
COOKING TIME: *2 hours*
SERVES 4–6

---

250 g haricot beans, soaked overnight
1 medium ham hock
2 onions, chopped
2 carrots, chopped
2 stalks celery, chopped
2 cloves garlic, crushed
2 bay leaves, crumbled
3 tomatoes peeled, seeded and chopped
¼ *cup tomato paste*
200 g spaghetti

1 Drain beans place in a large pan add ham hock, onions, carrots, celery, garlic and bay leaves. Add enough water to cover by 10–cm. Bring to the boil, reduce to a simmer, cover and cook for 1½ to 2 hours or until beans are tender.
2 Remove ham hock, cut meat from bone, discard skin fat and bone, shred meat and return to pot with tomatoes and tomato paste, bring back to the boil.
3 Add spaghetti cook until just tender. Serve with fresh crusty bread.
Note: Haricot beans are one of the many variety of white dried beans available from supermarkets or health food shops. When buying any of the white bean varieties look for smooth-skinned beans of good colour.

Risoni and Mushroom Broth

Avoid using large dark mushrooms for this recipe as they will give a grey colour to the soup. Choose medium pale caps. Wipe with damp absorbent paper before slicing, include stalks as they add flavour.

PREPARATION TIME: *15 minutes*
COOKING TIME: *10 minutes*
SERVES 4–6

90 g butter
2 cloves garlic, sliced
2 large onions, sliced
4 cups thinly sliced mushrooms
5 cups of chicken stock
125 g risoni
1¼ cups cream
extra 4 mushrooms sliced, cooked gently in butter until just soft, for garnish

1 Heat butter over a gentle heat until just melted. Add garlic and onions, cook

---

Pasta dishes are certainly simple to make and easy to enjoy. When cooking pasta dishes at home you need only a few basic pieces of equipment — firstly a large, deep-sided heavy pan for cooking the pasta, keep in mind that you need about 1 L of water to every 100 g of pasta. A second smaller pan is needed for simmering sauces and soups and a large heavy duty colander with a secure base is a must. Extra's include wooden spoons, slotted spoons and tongs or a pronged pasta scoop and a grater for Parmesan cheese.

1 minute, add mushrooms and allow to cook gently without colouring for 5 minutes. Add chicken stock and cook uncovered for 10 minutes.

2 While mushrooms are cooking add risoni to a large pan of boiling water and cook until just tender, drain and set aside.

3 Allow mushroom mixture to cool a little, then place in blender and blend for 3 minutes or until no large pieces of mushroom are evident.

4 Return mixture to pan, add risoni and cream, stir to combine. Heat gently until completely heated through, transfer to soup terrine or individual bowls, garnish with extra mushrooms.

Pea and Pasta Soup, Risoni and Mushroom Broth

Dried factory-made pasta, particularly durum wheat pasta which is the most superior, absorbs quite a large amount of water while cooking, it can swell three to four times it's size, especially short varieties like penne or farfalle. For this reason it must be cooked in a large pan of boiling water, with a little oil. When you add the pasta to the pan of boiling water (the water must be on a rolling boil) push it down with a long handled fork and stir the pasta so none sticks together or to the bottom of the pan. When you add nests of pasta take care to unravel the pasta strands in the water with a fork.

Fettucine and Eastern Style Salad

Flavours from the East combined with fettucine, spinach and carrot produce a tasty, easy to prepare salad. Tahini paste is available from health food stores.

PREPARATION TIME: *20 minutes*
COOKING TIME: *nil*
SERVES 4–6

1/3 cup currants
2 tablespoons lemon juice
250 g fettucine, cooked, drained and cooled
6 small spinach leaves, torn into pieces
2 carrots, coarsely grated
1/3 cup toasted pine nuts
1/2 cup plain yoghurt
1/2 cup orange juice
1 tablespoon tahini paste
freshly ground black pepper
3 tablespoons toasted sesame seeds

1 Soak currants in lemon juice for about 10 minutes to plump.
2 Place fettucine, spinach, carrots, currants and pine nuts in a large bowl. Combine yoghurt, orange juice, tahini paste and black pepper, mix well to combine.
3 Pour dressing over fettucine mixture, toss well to combine. Place onto large serving platter sprinkle with sesame seeds.

Penne Pasta and Butter Bean Salad

Any cooked cold tube or spiral pasta can be used for this recipe. Proscuitto is an Italian ham available from most delicatessens. Because of its strong flavour it is cut into paper thin slices.

PREPARATION TIME: *10 minutes*
COOKING TIME: *nil*
SERVES 4–6

300 g penne, cooked and cooled
1/4 cup lemon juice
2 teaspoons grated lemon rind

1/3 cup olive oil
2 tablespoons chopped basil
freshly ground black pepper
1 × 310 g can butter beans, drained
200 g proscuitto, sliced diagonally
1 small red capsicum, sliced diagonally
basil sprigs, for garnish (optional)

1 Place pasta into large bowl and add combined lemon juice, rind, olive oil, basil and black pepper. Toss to combine.
2 Add beans, proscuitto and capsicum. Toss to combine. Transfer to large bowl, garnish with basil and serve.
Note: This salad can also be served in individual plates as a starter to a meal or as a larger main course serving.

Spiral Pasta Salad with Tomatoes, Olives and Feta

Quick, easy to make salad. Ideal as a meal on its own or as an accompaniment to grilled fish or chicken. Penne pasta could be used in place of spiral.

PREPARATION TIME: *10 minutes*
COOKING TIME: *nil*
SERVES 4–6

1/3 cup olive oil
1/4 cup white vinegar
2 tablespoons tomato juice
freshly ground black pepper
1/4 cup chopped fresh dill
250 g spiral pasta, cooked, well drained and cooled
5 small firm ripe tomatoes, cut into wedges
125 g black olives,
200 g feta cheese, crumbled
2 small white onions, peeled and sliced thinly

1 Combine olive oil, vinegar, tomato juice, black pepper and fresh dill in screw top jar, shake until well mixed.
2 Place pasta into a large bowl, add dressing, tomatoes, olives, cheese and onions. Mix gently to combine.
3 Serve on large serving plates.

Spiral Pasta Salad with Tomatoes, Olives and Feta, Tagliatelle with Vegetable Ribbons and Walnut Sauce (page 11)   13

Left: Penne Pasta and
Butter Bean Salad (page
12), Pappardelle Bake

Pappardelle Bake

Lentils are available in green, brown or red
but only the red can be used without
soaking. This dish can be constructed 2–3
days before required, refrigerated and
baked when needed. Penne or rigatoni can
be used in place of pappardelle.

PREPARATION TIME: *40 minutes*
COOKING TIME: *30 minutes*
SERVES 4–6

When cooking baked
pasta dishes coat the
base of the baking
dish with a little
sauce and or oil for
ease of cutting and
serving. Before baking
cover the completed
dish loosely with
aluminium foil. Bake
as directed, remove
foil 10 minutes
before completed
cooking time to give
a moist pasta dish a
golden top.

2 tablespoons oil
2 onions chopped
1 clove garlic, crushed
2 sticks celery, chopped
4 large tomatoes, peeled and chopped
2½ cups chicken stock
1 cup red lentils
200 g pappardelle
60 g butter
200g small mushrooms, cut in half
½ cup fresh breadcrumbs
CREAM SAUCE
60 g butter

¼ cup plain flour
2 cups milk
¼ cup cream
1 egg

1 Place oil in pan, add onion, garlic and
celery cook gently until golden brown.
Add tomatoes and chicken stock, bring to
the boil. Add lentils, cook for 25 minutes
or until lentils are tender and most of the
liquid has evaporated.
2 Cook pasta in pan of boiling water until
just tender. Drain and set aside. Melt
butter in small pan, add mushrooms cook
gently until just soft.
3 To make sauce: melt butter in pan
remove from heat blend in flour return to
heat, cook 2 minutes without colouring.
Remove from heat, gradually stir in milk,
return to heat, stir constantly until mixture boils and thickens. Combine cream
and egg mixture into sauce mixture.
4 Place cooked pappardelle into well
greased ovenproof dish, top with lentil
mixture and then mushrooms. Pour over
cream sauce. Sprinkle with breadcrumbs.
Bake at 180°C for 25–30 minutes until
heated through and sauce has risen slightly
and is golden brown.

Pasta Pie

Pasta in a cheese sauce enclosed in puff pastry, makes an ideal winter evening meal. Penne pasta is used in this recipe, any small cooked pasta can be substituted. Serve accompanied by a crisp green salad.

PREPARATION TIME: *15 minutes plus cooling time*
COOKING TIME: *40 minutes*
SERVES 4

60 g butter
½ small red capsicum, chopped
1 onion, chopped
⅓ cup plain flour
1½ cups milk
¼ teaspoon nutmeg
½ cup frozen peas, thawed
125 g Gouda cheese, grated
1 cup cooked, cooled penne
2 sheets ready rolled shortcrust pastry
1 egg, lightly beaten for glazing

1 Melt butter over gentle heat, add capsicum and onion cook without colouring until capsicum and onion are soft. Remove from heat add flour, stir to combine. Gradually stir in milk, add nutmeg, return to the heat stir constantly until mixture boils and thickens.
2 Stir in cheese, peas and pasta mix gently to combine. Cool completely before placing on pastry.
3 Cut into 1 × 20–cm round of pastry for base and 1 × 24–cm for top. Place base pastry onto well greased flat baking tray. Place cooled filling mounted in centre, glaze 3–cm from outer edge.
4 Place top pastry over base, press down on glazed section to seal. Glaze top, cut small hole in top and place a small cone shaped piece of aluminium foil point end into hole. This will allow steam to escape and prevent pastry from becoming soggy. Bake at 200°C for 12 minutes reduce temperature to 180°C cook for 25–30 minutes longer. Pastry should be well risen and dark golden brown. Serve immediately.

Carefully spoon the cooled pasta filling into the centre of pastry base.

Use a pastry brush dipped in lightly beaten egg to glaze outer edge of pastry base.

Use two fingers as shown to pinch a decorative edge around pie.

Pasta Pie

When cooking pasta, start timing immediately after the water returns to boil, stir for 1–2 minutes to prevent pasta sticking together.

Ricotta Filled Ravioli with Fresh Tomato Sauce

This recipe makes an ideal entrée. Dough can be rolled using a pasta machine, it can also be cut into 4–cm rounds, filled and folded over to make half moon shapes, seal edges. Cook as per recipe.

PREPARATION TIME: *45 minutes plus 30 minutes standing time*
COOKING TIME: *7–10 minutes*
SERVES 4–6

RAVIOLI DOUGH
1 cup plain flour
1 egg
1 tablespoon oil
1 teaspoon water
FILLING
500 g ricotta cheese
125 g prosciutto
1 tablespoon Italian parsley
1 egg yolk
SAUCE
1 tablespoon oil
1 onion chopped
2 cloves garlic, crushed
1 carrot, chopped
1 kg ripe tomatoes, skinned and chopped
50 g tomato paste
1 teaspoon brown sugar
½ cup chicken stock
1 tablespoon Worcestershire sauce
½ cup chopped fresh basil

1 To make ravioli dough: sift flour into a bowl. Make well in centre and add egg, oil and water, gradually incorporate into flour. Turn out onto slightly floured board, knead until smooth and elastic. Cover and stand for 30 minutes.
2 Prepare filling while pastry is resting. Combine ricotta, prosciutto, parsley and egg yolk. Mix well.
3 Prepare sauce while pastry is resting. Place oil in a large heavy based pan. Add onion, garlic and carrot. Gently cook 5–7 minutes. Add tomato paste, sugar, stock, Worcestershire sauce and basil. Bring to the boil, reduce to simmer, cover, cook 30 minutes. Purée mixture in blender, keep warm.
4 Halve dough, reshape each piece into smooth ball. Roll out each portion thinly to a long oblong shape. Place teaspoons of filling in mounds at 5–cm intervals in regular lines on one sheet of dough. Brush between mounds of filling with water, place other sheet of dough carefully over top. Press down between filling to seal. Use a pastry wheel or knife to cut into squares.
5 Drop ravioli into pan of boiling water cook 8–10 minutes or until tender. Remove ravioli from water using slotted spoon place into heated serving dish, cover with sauce. Serve immediately.

Fettucine with Red Pesto

Red pesto is a tangy cold sauce that will coat hot pasta beautifully. Red pimento is available in jars or cans from supermarkets or delicatessens. Pesto can be made and stored in covered container in refrigerator 3–4 days.

PREPARATION TIME:
7 minutes plus 30 minutes soaking time
COOKING TIME: *10 minutes*
SERVES 4–6

350 g fettucine
200 g red pimento, drained and coarsely chopped
1 tomato, peeled and seeded
6 anchovies, soaked in milk for 30 minutes
⅓ cup pine nuts
1 tablespoon dried breadcrumbs
1 tablespoon capers
1 tablespoon red wine vinegar
½ cup olive oil

1 Cook fettucine in a large pan of boiling water until just tender.
2 While pasta is cooking: place pimento, tomato, anchovies, pine nuts and bread-crumbs into food processor. Process until a paste is formed.
3 Add capers and red wine vinegar and blend for 1 minute. Add oil gradually until a soft paste is formed.
4 Drain fettucine mix pesto through hot pasta. Serve immediately. Garnish with extra pinenuts and capers, if desired.

Small squares or round envelopes of pasta filled with eggs and various cheeses, are traditionally known as ravioli. Meat filled ravioli are known as agnolotti. Although today, we associate ravioli as a filled pasta with any combination of filling: be it with eggs, cheese, vegetables or meat.

Many years ago in Liguria (Northern Italy), ravioli was invented chiefly to use up leftover food. The original name for the filled envelopes or pillows was *rabioli* which translated means bits and pieces. Today we recognise this pasta as ravioli and do not necessarily make them to use up leftover food.

Clockwise from left: Farfalle Pasta and Vegetable Salad (page 18), Ricotta Filled Ravioli with Fresh Tomato Sauce, Fettucine with Red Pesto

Is there a correct way to eat pasta? There are two schools of thought about this, one says that it's best to catch a few strands of pasta on a fork, then with the tines resting in the bowl of a spoon twist the fork against the spoon to roll up the pasta. The other method is to spear a few strands on a fork and rest the fork against the plate twirling the fork to catch the pasta. Either way is acceptable, use whatever technique works for you.

Farfalle Pasta and Vegetable Salad

Easy to make colourful salad consisting of farfalle (bow) pasta and a vegetable medley combined with tangy mustard dressing. Try a medium shell pasta in place of bow.

PREPARATION TIME: 10–12 minutes
COOKING TIME: nil
SERVES 4–6

250 g bow pasta
250 g broccoli, broken into florets
250 g beans, cut diagonally
125 g snow peas, topped and tailed
1 punnet cherry tomatoes, halved
1/3 cup olive oil
1/4 cup white wine vinegar
2 teaspoons dry mustard powder
1 teaspoon tumeric
freshly ground black pepper
1 punnet snow pea sprouts

1 Cook pasta in a large quantity of boiling water until just tender. Drain well in cold water and set aside.
2 Plunge broccoli, beans and snow peas into boiling water. Drain immediately in cold water and allow to stand. Wash tomatoes and set aside.
3 Combine olive oil, vinegar, mustard, tumeric and black pepper, beat well with a fork.
4 Add pasta, vegetables and dressing, toss well to combine. Place into serving bowl, top with sprouts.

Shell Pasta with Olive Sauce

A creamy salty flavoured sauce thickened by the addition of breadcrumbs rather than flour. A combination of black and green olives attributes to the unique saltiness. Penne pasta could be used in place of shell.

PREPARATION TIME: 15 minutes
COOKING TIME: 5 minutes
SERVES 4–6

400 g small shell pasta
30 g butter
2 cloves garlic, crushed
1/4 cup fresh dried breadcrumbs
1/4 cup finely chopped pecans
125 g black olives, stoned, finely chopped
125 g green olives, stoned, finely chopped
1/2 cup cream
extra 1/2 cup roughly chopped pecans

1 Cook pasta in large pan of boiling water, until just tender.
2 While pasta is cooking: melt butter in a large pan, add garlic and breadcrumbs, stir until golden brown. Add pecans, cook 1 minute longer. Add olives stirring 2–3 minutes until mixture is well mixed.
3 Add wine, cook 1 minute. Stir in cream cook for 30 seconds.
4 Drain cooked pasta, add to sauce mixture toss well to combine. Place onto heated serving dish, top with extra pecans. Serve immediately.

Chilli Pappardelle with Cream Sauce

A different, but perfect combination of flavours. The heat of the chilli is mellowed by the cream sauce. Adjust the amount of chilli to suit your personal taste. Fettucine may be used in place of pappardelle.

PREPARATION TIME: 8–10 minutes
COOKING TIME: 3–4 minutes
SERVE 4–6

400 g pappardelle
50 g unsalted butter
1 cup cream
200 g fresh Parmesan cheese, grated
1 tablespoon olive oil
1 small red chilli, cut into fine shreds
2–3 drops of chilli oil
1/2 teaspoon paprika

1 Cook pappardelle in boiling water until just tender.
2 While pasta is cooking: melt butter in pan, do not allow to brown. Add cream and cheese, heat gently for 4–5 minutes.

3 In a separate pan heat olive oil, add chilli, chilli oil and paprika, cook 2–3 minutes. Drain pappardelle, add to chilli mixture, toss well to combine.

4 Place pappardelle onto heated serving dish, pour over cream sauce. Serve immediately.

Note: It is advisable to protect your hands with plastic gloves when preparing chillies. Try using scissors to chop, instead of a knife, it makes the job much easier.

Pasta Stuffed Capsicum

A combination of red, green and yellow capsicum was chosen for this recipe. Anchovies can be purchased in brine or oil. To remove excess salt soak in a little milk before using. For a brown top to the capsicum cook without covering.

PREPARATION TIME: *30 minutes*
COOKING TIME: *40 minutes*
SERVES 4–6

250 g macaroni
6 large equal-sized capsicum
1 tablespoon olive oil
100 g black olives, stoned and chopped
100 g sun dried tomatoes, chopped
4 anchovy fillets, chopped
1 teaspoon capers, chopped
2 tablespoons tomato paste
2 teaspoon brown sugar
200 g mozzarella cheese, coarsely grated

1 Cook macaroni in boiling water for 6 minutes only. Drain and set aside.

2 Cut tops, stem end from capsicum remove seeds and white membrane being careful not to pierce the capsicum. Do not discard tops.

3 Place oil into pan, add olives, tomatoes, anchovies, capers, tomato paste and brown sugar cook over low heat 2–3 minute, stir to combine. Remove from heat, stir in macaroni and cheese.

4 Fill capsicum with macaroni mixture. Place into greased baking dish. Place tops back on capsicum. Bake at 180°C for 30–40 minutes.

Rigatoni and Broccoli with Cauliflower Sauce

Pasta and broccoli topped with creamy cauliflower sauce, sprinkled with toasted almonds is perfect as a meal on its own or as an accompaniment. Do not overcook broccoli, it should be bright green in colour and crisp to the bite.

PREPARATION TIME: *30 minutes*
COOKING TIME: *10 minutes*
SERVES 4–6

2 tablespoons olive oil
2 cloves garlic, crushed
500 g cauliflower, cut into florets
1 cup chicken stock
½ cup white wine
500 g rigatoni
250 g broccoli, cut into florets
1 cup cream
⅓ cup flaked almonds, toasted

1 Place olive oil in pan, add garlic, cook gently 2 minutes. Add cauliflower cook 5 minutes. Add chicken stock and wine, cover and cook until cauliflower is very tender.

2 While cauliflower is cooking: add rigatoni to large pan of boiling water, cook until just tender. Cook broccoli in boiling water for 4 minutes. Drain and keep warm.

3 Mash cauliflower in pan with stock using a potato masher. Add cream and simmer for 5 minutes. Drain rigatoni. Add broccoli to rigatoni toss to combine place onto large serving dish.

4 Pour sauce over rigatoni and broccoli, sprinkle with almonds and serve.

For an almost instant pasta sauce simply combine freshly squeezed lemon juice finely chopped parsley and garlic, toss through hot or cold pasta.

Rigatoni and Broccoli with Cauliflower Sauce

Rigatoni with Minted Zucchini

Zucchinis are covered in salt and allowed to stand to remove excess moisture. Make sure they are rinsed well in cold water and dried very well before cooking. Zucchini sticks can be deep-fried or shallow-fried, drain on absorbent paper before using.

PREPARATION TIME: *20 minutes plus 30 minutes standing time*
COOKING TIME: *15 minutes*
SERVES 4–6

1 kg zucchinis, washed and trimmed
2 tablespoons salt
400 g rigatoni
vegetable oil, for frying
1/3 cup olive oil
1/3 cup white wine
1/4 cup roughly chopped mint
1 clove garlic, crushed
freshly ground black pepper

1 Cut zucchini into sticks approximately 5-cm long × 5-mm thick. Place zucchini sticks into colander, add salt toss well. Place colander over bowl let stand for 30 minutes.
2 Rinse zucchini in cold water, dry well with absorbent paper. Place vegetable oil in a large pan until moderately hot. Cook the zucchini in small batches until golden brown. Place zucchini in large bowl add olive oil, vinegar, mint, garlic and black pepper.
3 Place rigatoni in large pan of boiling water, cook until just tender.
4 Drain rigatoni, add to zucchini, toss well to combine. Serve immediately.

Rigatoni with Minted Zucchini

Olive oil was used many years ago by the ancient Greeks, Spaniards and Romans both for cooking purposes and as a fuel to provide light. Today, olive oil is still present in almost every Greek, Spanish and Italian home, but used for cooking purposes only. Thanks to technology, other power and heating resources have been made available to us eliminating the need of olive oil as a fuel.

Macaroni Soufflé

Pasta suspended in a soufflé mixture flavoured with sun dried tomatoes. Sun dried tomatoes have a unique flavour, fresh tomatoes cannot be substituted.

PREPARATION TIME: *20 minutes*
COOKING TIME: *35 minutes*
SERVES 4–6

500 g medium sized shell pasta
4 zucchinis, halved and sliced
125 g sun dried tomatoes, roughly chopped
2 tablespoons olive oil
60 g butter
1/3 cup plain flour
1 1/2 cups milk
3/4 cup freshly grated Parmesan cheese
4 egg yolks
6 egg whites

1 Boil pasta in a large quantity of boiling water 8 minutes only, drain set aside. Heat oil in pan, add zucchinis cook until golden brown, add tomatoes cook for 2 minutes set aside.
2 Melt butter in pan over low heat, remove from heat stir in flour gradually, add milk and return to heat stirring until mixture boils and thickens. Stir in cheese and egg yolks.
3 Combine pasta, zucchini, tomatoes and white sauce. Beat egg whites until soft peaks are formed, gently fold into pasta mixture.
4 Place the mixture into a large greased soufflé or straight sided casserole dish. Bake at 180°C until well risen and golden brown. Serve immediately.
Note: This delicious pasta dish does not rise quite as high as a true soufflé. The final result is a puffy, lightly golden dish with a creamy, moist centre. Take care when folding the egg whites into the pasta mixture to ensure maximum volume and lightness.

Macaroni Soufflé, Spaghetti with Lemon Cream Sauce (page 22)

21

Spaghetti with Lemon Cream Sauce

This dish makes an ideal start to any meal or as part of a summer or winter luncheon.

PREPARATION TIME: 40 minutes
COOKING TIME: 8–10 minutes
SERVES 4–6

30 g butter
1 clove garlic, crushed
2 lemons, rind removed
2 cups cream
500 g spaghetti
extra lemon rind, cut in long shreds for garnish
freshly ground black pepper

1 Melt butter in pan, add garlic cook gently 2–3 minutes. Add lemon rind and cream cook over gentle heat for 30–40 minutes or until sauce has reduced by 1/3.
2 Cook spaghetti until just tender in boiling water. Drain.
3 Combine spaghetti and sauce there should be just enough sauce to coat the spaghetti.
4 Place spaghetti and sauce onto heated serving platter garnish with extra lemon rind and pepper.

> Pasta is best served as soon as cooked. However, it can be kept hot by either returning drained cooked pasta to the empty cooking pan, adding 2 tablespoons of oil and covering to keep warm; or draining pasta in colander and setting over pan containing small amount of simmering water.

Pasta with Mushroom Pesto

Fresh mushrooms are used in this recipe, in Italy the dried mushroom *porcini* is often used. This type of mushroom can be difficult to obtain, do not substitute Chinese dried mushrooms as they have a completely different flavour. Tagliatelle may be used in place of spaghetti.

PREPARATION TIME: 30 minutes
COOKING TIME: 15 minutes
SERVES 4–6

60 g butter
1/4 cup olive oil
400 g mushroom caps, medium-size,
wiped with damp cloth and finely chopped
1 onion, finely chopped
1/4 cup pine nuts, chopped
2 cloves garlic, crushed
1 tablespoon fresh rosemary leaves, finely chopped
1 × 450 g can tomatoes, well drained, finely chopped
400 g spaghetti
extra 1/3 cup pine nuts, toasted (optional)

1 Place butter and oil in pan heating over gentle heat. Add mushrooms, onions, pine nuts, garlic and rosemary, cook gently for 15 minutes stirring occasionally.
2 Add tomatoes, cook gently for 10 minutes longer. Place spaghetti into a large pan of boiling water, cook until just tender. Drain, place back into pan, mix in mushroom pesto.
3 Place on large heated serving dish, sprinkle with extra toasted pine nuts. Serve immediately.

Spinach Crêpes filled with Macaroni Cheese

Crêpes can be made beforehand and either refrigerated or frozen until required. Sauce can be made 2–3 days before needed. Small shell pasta can be used in place of macaroni.

PREPARATION TIME: 50 minutes
COOKING TIME: 15 minutes
SERVES 4

CREPES
1 1/4 cups flour
1 1/4 cups milk
2 eggs
1/2 cup thawed frozen spinach
FILLING
60g tablespoons butter
1/3 cup plain flour
1 1/2 cups milk
1/4 cup grated Parmesan cheese
1/2 cup grated Cheddar cheese
2 cups cooked, cooled macaroni
SAUCE
2 tablespoons olive oil
2 cloves garlic
1 onion chopped

*1 red capsicum, seeds, membrane and
skin removed
3 large ripe tomatoes, skin and seeds
removed
2 teaspoons sugar
2 teaspoons red wine vinegar*

1 To make crêpes: combine all ingredients
in blender or food processor. Process until
batter is smooth. Heat a small crêpe pan
over a medium heat. Lightly oil pan. Pour
2–3 tablespoons of crêpe mixture into
pan, turn or swirl pan so mixture covers
base of pan evenly. When crêpe is lightly
brown underneath, carefully lift and cook
other side. Repeat with remaining mixture
until you have eight crêpes. Allow to cool
before using.

2 To prepare filling: melt butter in pan
and remove from heat, stir in flour gradually, add milk and return to heat stirring
constantly until mixture boils and
thickens. Add cheese and macaroni, stir
gently to combine. Set aside.
3 To prepare sauce: heat oil in pan add
garlic and onion, cook 2–3 minutes. Add
capsicum, tomatoes, sugar and vinegar
cover and cook for 15 minutes. While
sauce is cooking fill crêpes with macaroni
mixture. Place crêpes in lightly greased
ovenproof dish.
4 Place cooked sauce mixture in blender,
blend on high until smooth. Spoon sauce
down centre of crêpes. Cover and cook at
180°C for 15 minutes or until heated
through.

*Spinach Crêpes filled
with Macaroni Cheese,
Pasta with Mushroom
Pesto*

23

PASTA SHAPES AND SIZES

Pasta comes in a diverse range of shapes and sizes, the names given to each type differ from region to region. The smallest difference in width or thickness may give pasta yet another name. In fact there are hundreds of named pasta shapes, to add to the confusion. Here we show you the dried and fresh pasta shapes used in this book and the names used for each.

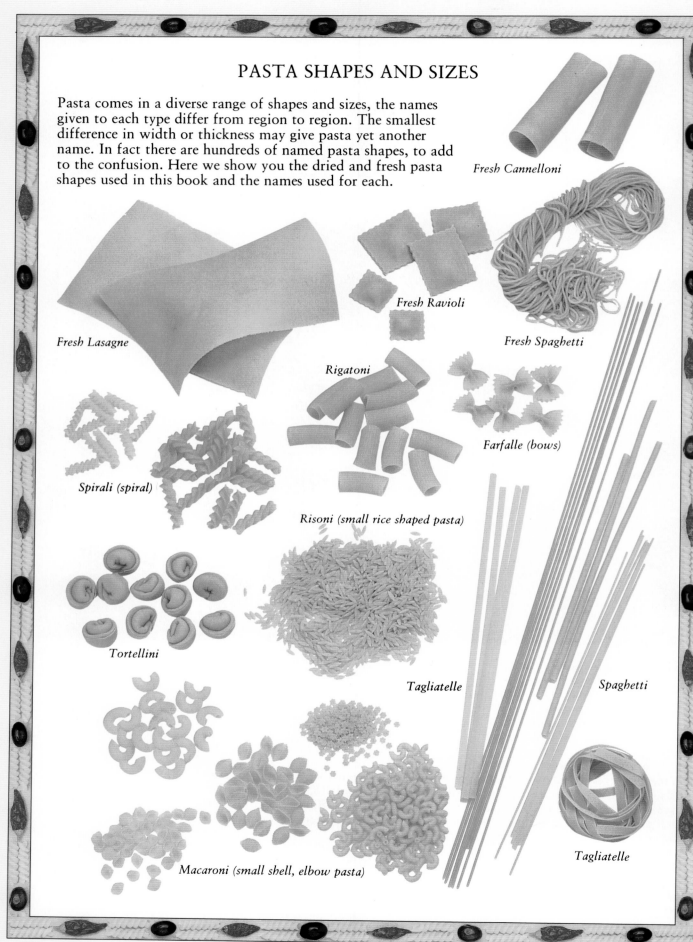

Fresh Cannelloni

Fresh Ravioli

Fresh Spaghetti

Fresh Lasagne

Rigatoni

Farfalle (bows)

Spirali (spiral)

Risoni (small rice shaped pasta)

Tortellini

Tagliatelle

Spaghetti

Macaroni (small shell, elbow pasta)

Tagliatelle

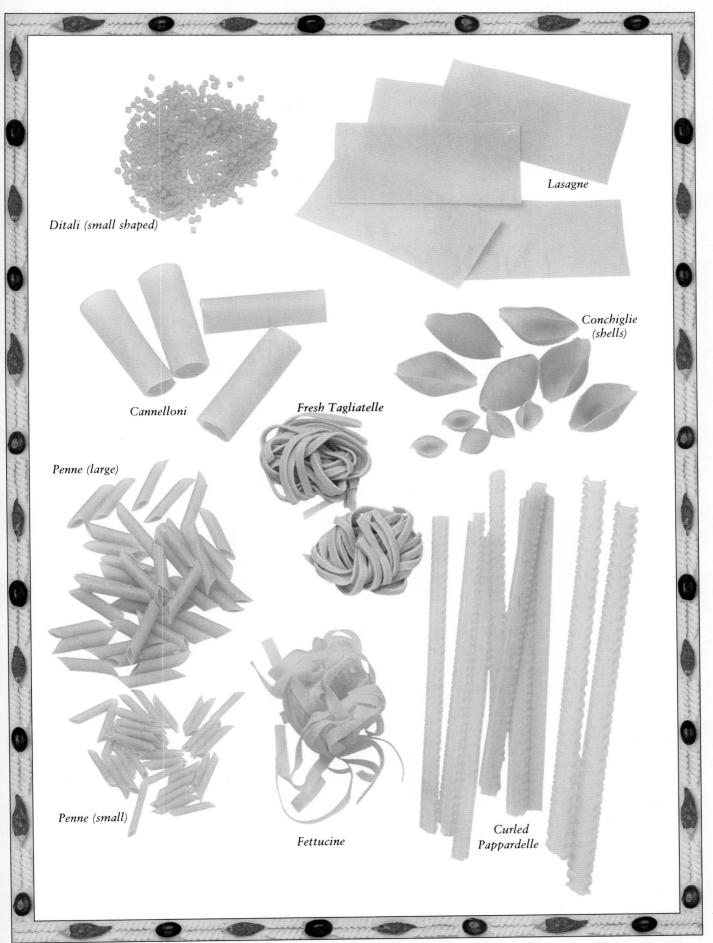

Ditali (small shaped)

Lasagne

Cannelloni

Fresh Tagliatelle

Conchiglie
(shells)

Penne (large)

Penne (small)

Fettucine

Curled
Pappardelle

Noodles with Seasonal Vegetables

A GREAT VARIETY OF fresh and dried noodles are available, they can be made from wheat or rice flour or mung bean starch. Noodle shapes do not vary as much as pasta, they may be thin or thick, flat or rounded. The Asian noodle-maker applies a skill that has been practised for over 1500 years. In the hands of a skilled noodle-maker the lengths of the noodles remain unbroken, this is seen as a symbol of long life.

This medley of delicious noodle and vegetable dishes is certainly a splendid collection, there's something here for everyone. Try the simple delight of Egg Noodle and Roasted Capsicum Salad or the Asian inspired Somen Noodle and Vegetable Soup. Anyone who relishes hot and spicy dishes will certainly enjoy Chilli Noodle and Cashew Stir-Fry or the zesty Chilli Satay Noodles.

Chilli Noodle and Cashew Stir-Fry (page 28), Somen Noodle Vegetable Soup (page 28)

Noodle and Mixed Vegetable Soup

Use any combination of vegetables for this soup. We have chosen to use Chinese cabbage, cauliflower and green beans. The soup is best made close to serving time.

PREPARATION TIME: *15 minutes*
COOKING TIME: *15 minutes*
SERVES 4

1 tablespoon oil
1 onion, finely chopped
1 clove garlic, crushed
1 cup finely shredded Chinese cabbage
200 g cauliflower, chopped
4 cups beef stock
125 g dried wheat noodles
100 g green beans, cut into 2-cm lengths
¼ teaspoon Chinese five spice powder
1 tablespoon light soy sauce
1 egg, lightly beaten
spring onion, chopped (optional)

1 Heat oil in pan. Add onion and garlic, stir over medium heat 5 minutes. Add cabbage, cauliflower and stock, bring to boil. Add noodles, reduce heat, simmer uncovered 5 minutes, stir occasionally.
2 Stir in beans, spice and soy sauce, simmer further 5 minutes or until beans and noodles are tender.
3 Stir in egg, remove from heat, continue to stir until egg forms thin strands. Serve soup sprinkled with chopped spring onions.

Somen noodles are Japanese in origin and made from ground buckwheat and wheat flour. They are beige or coloured with green tea which also gives the noodles a subtle flavour. These popular noodles are served cold with a soy dipping sauce and topped with thin pieces of vegetables or seafood.

Somen Noodle and Vegetable Soup

This unique noodle and vegetable soup has a strong Japanese influence. The somen noodles, oyster mushrooms and nori are but a few of their favourite and more commonly used ingredients.

PREPARATION TIME: *20 minutes*
COOKING TIME: *15 minutes*
SERVES 4

4 cups clear fish stock
1 teaspoon finely grated ginger
3 oyster mushrooms
1 tablespoon soy sauce or rice vinegar
1 tablespoon oyster sauce
100 g dried bundle Japanese somen noodles
100 g snow peas, thinly sliced
½ sheet nori (seaweed), cut into fine shreds
100 g tofu, cut into 1.5-cm cubes (optional)
spring onion, shredded (optional)

1 Bring fish stock to the boil, reduce heat to low, add ginger, mushrooms, sauces and somen noodles. Stir over a low heat 10 minutes.
2 Add snow peas and nori; stir 2 minutes or until peas are tender. Spoon soup into warmed bowls and garnish with tofu and spring onion shreds, if desired.
Note: Pickled ginger may be used in place of the green ginger. It is available from Asian grocery stores, and has a pleasant sweet ginger flavour and crunchy texture.

Chilli Noodle and Cashew Stir-Fry

Here's a rather hot and highly flavoursome chilli stir-fry, ideal for those who enjoy spicy, hot food. The recipe is best made close to serving and is not suitable to freeze or microwave. Use less chillies if desired.

PREPARATION TIME: *10 minutes*
COOKING TIME: *5 minutes*
SERVES 4

200 g thin noodles, chopped
¼ cup oil
2 teaspoons chilli oil
3 small red chillies, pounded
½ cup unsalted, roasted cashew nuts
1 red capsicum, sliced diagonally
2 sticks celery, sliced diagonally
225 g can whole baby corn, drained
100 g bean sprouts
1 tablespoon soy sauce
2 tablespoons Thai sweet chilli sauce
2 tablespoons chopped spring onions

1 Cook noodles in large pan of simmering water until just tender; drain.
2 Heat oils in wok or pan, add chillies, cook over medium heat 1 minute. Add cashews, toss 1 minute or until golden.
3 Add vegetables to pan, cook over medium heat 3 minutes or until vegetables are tender. Stir in noodles and combined sauces. Toss until noodles are heated through and all ingredients are combined. Serve immediately sprinkled with spring onions.

Fruity Noodle Salad

This salad looks most appealing if arranged on a serving platter and drizzled with the dressing just before serving. Do not prepare too far ahead as the pear may discolour.

PREPARATION TIME: *15 minutes*
COOKING TIME: *nil*
SERVES 4–6

125 g flat wheat noodles
1 small pear, peeled, chopped
1 cup finely chopped red cabbage
1 stick celery, thinly sliced
¼ cup chopped pecan nuts
1 orange, segmented
DRESSING
2 tablespoons sour cream
2 teaspoons mayonnaise
1 tablespoon prepared French dressing
1 tablespoon finely chopped basil

1 Cook noodles in large pan of boiling water until just tender; drain, cool.
2 Combine noodles, pear, cabbage, celery and nuts together in a bowl, toss until mixed.
3 Transfer salad to serving platter. Arrange orange segments over salad. Pour dressing over just before serving.
4 To make dressing: beat cream, mayonnaise, dressing and basil together in a jug until combined.

Curry Flavoured Noodles

A mild curry coats the noodles and vegetables in this recipe. It is a simple dish to prepare with minimal fuss and preparation.

PREPARATION TIME: *25 minutes*
COOKING TIME: *10 minutes*
SERVES 4

250 g thick fresh noodles
¼ cup oil
2 cloves garlic, sliced
1 onion, finely sliced
1 red capsicum, cut into thin 4–cm long strips
1 small cucumber, unpeeled, cut into thin 4–cm strips
2 teaspoons mild curry powder
½ cup chicken stock
2 teaspoons dry sherry
1 tablespoon soy sauce
½ teaspoon sugar
3 spring onions, chopped

1 Cook noodles in large pan of boiling water until just tender; drain.
2 Heat oil in wok or pan. Add garlic, onion and red capsicum, stir over medium heat 3 minutes. Add cucumber and curry powder, stir over medium heat a further 3 minutes.
3 Add combined stock, sherry, soy sauce and sugar, stir until mixture boils. Add noodles and spring onions, stir over low heat 3 minutes or until ingredients are well combined and heated through.

In Asia noodles are eaten day and night, at home, in restaurants and at food stalls. The Chinese produce large sheets of fresh rice noodle made with a mixture of rice flour, wheat starch and flour. This mixture is poured onto a steamer plate and steamed in thin sheets. Prawns, pork or vegetable are used as fillings for the noodle, they are generally served with a thin oyster sauce and sesame oil.

Curry Flavoured Noodles

Fresh Noodle and Bean Toss

The word noodle developed from the German and Austrian word for dumpling, *nudeln knodel.* Dumplings originated from the habit of dropping small pieces of uncooked dough into soups and stews. Today near to every country around the world has their own particular type of noodle and or dumpling.

Not all noodle recipes must be served with an oriental influence. In this recipe the combination of noodles and vegetables are complemented with a subtle creamy, dill flavoured sauce. Serve fresh egg noodle and bean toss for lunch or as an accompaniment to a main meal.

PREPARATION TIME: *10 minutes*
COOKING TIME: *10 minutes*
SERVES 4

250 g thin fresh wheat noodles
2 tablespoons oil
1 onion, sliced
2 cloves garlic, crushed
100 g green beans, chopped
2 tomatoes, peeled, chopped
2 tablespoons fruit chutney
310 g red kidney beans, rinsed, drained
½ cup cream
1 tablespoon chopped fresh dill

1 Cook noodles in large pan of boiling water until just tender; drain.
2 Heat oil in pan or wok. Add onion, garlic and beans. Toss over high heat 2 minutes. Reduce heat, add tomatoes, chutney and kidney beans to pan, cook over medium heat 2 minutes.
3 Add noodles to vegetables, mix well. Stir in cream and dill, toss until combined. Serve immediately.
Note: Do not make this dish too far in advance as the cream will be absorbed causing the noodles to dry out.

Chilli Satay Noodles

Try this wonderfully hot and nutty noodle dish with your friends. It will be a hit every time.

PREPARATION TIME: *10 minutes*
COOKING TIME: *10 minutes*
SERVES 4–6

500 g thin fresh egg noodles
1 tablespoon oil
1 teaspoon sesame oil
⅓ cup peanuts, shelled, peeled
2 small red chillies
4 thin eggplants, sliced
200 g sugar snap peas
100 g bean sprouts
¼ cup crunchy peanut butter
1 tablespoon Hoi Sin sauce
⅓ cup coconut milk
2 tablespoons lime juice
1 tablespoon Thai sweet chilli sauce

1 Cook noodles in large pan of boiling water until just tender; drain.
2 Heat oils in wok or pan. Add peanuts, toss over high heat 1 minute or until golden. Add chillies, eggplant and sugar snap peas to pan, cook over high heat 2 minutes, reduce heat to medium.
3 Add noodles and sprouts to pan, toss 1 minute or until combined.
4 Blend peanut butter, Hoi Sin sauce, coconut milk, lime juice and chilli sauce in a jug until almost smooth. Pour into noodle mixture in pan. Toss over medium heat until noodles are well coated and sauce has heated through. Serve immediately.
Note: Thai sweet chilli is a red, semi transparent sweet sauce with a hint of chilli.

Noodle and Lettuce Salad with Croûtons

A light and refreshing summer salad with a mediterranean influence.

PREPARATION TIME: *12 minutes*
COOKING TIME: *5 minutes*
SERVES 4

125 g thick egg noodles, cut into 5–cm lengths
1 tablespoon butter
1 thick slice bread, crust removed, cut into 1–cm cubes
½ butterhead lettuce, torn into bite-size pieces
60 g feta cheese, crumbled
¼ cup black olives
½ cup sun dried tomatoes, drained

Above: Noodle and Lettuce Salad with Croûtons; Below: Fresh Noodle and Bean Toss

DRESSING
1 tablespoon red wine vinegar
1/4 cup olive oil
1/2 teaspoon dried oregano leaves
2 cloves garlic, crushed
1/2 teaspoon mustard powder
1/2 teaspoon brown sugar

1 Cook noodles in large pan of boiling water until just tender; drain.
2 Heat butter in pan. Add bread cubes, cook over low heat **5** minutes or until cubes are golden all over; drain on absorbent paper.
3 Arrange lettuce leaves over base of serving platter, top with noodles. Sprinkle with feta, olives, and sun dried tomatoes. Top with croûtons.
4 Pour dressing over salad just before serving.
5 To make dressing: shake all ingredients together in a jar with a tight fitting lid.

Egg Noodle and Roasted Capsicum Salad

The combination of roasted red and green capsicum with fresh noodles and the mint dressing is exquisitely light and refreshing. The salad is particularly appropriate for a dinner party or other special occasions. Recipe is best made a day ahead to allow the flavours to develop.

PREPARATION TIME: *10 minutes plus 10 minutes standing time*
COOKING TIME: *20 minutes*
SERVES 4

250 g fresh thick egg noodles
2 red capsicums, seeded, cut into quarters
2 green capsicums, seeded, cut into quarters
1 large carrot, cut into fine strips, 6–cm long
3 spring onions, chopped
1/3 cup olive oil
2 tablespoons lemon juice
1 tablespoon finely chopped fresh mint

1 Cook noodles in large pan of boiling water until just tender; drain, cool.
2 Place capsicum on foil-lined oven tray, skin side up. Grill at medium heat for 20 minutes or until skins blister and burn. Remove from grill, cover with clean damp tea-towel, stand 10 minutes.
3 Carefully remove skins from capsicum. Cut flesh into 1–cm wide strips. Place capsicum in bowl with noodles, carrot and spring onions, toss until just combined.
4 Whisk oil, lemon and mint together in small jug. Pour over salad, mix well. Cover, refrigerate several hours or over-night. Toss again just before serving.
Note: Drained, canned pimentos may be used in this recipe if desired, but the full roasted flavour will not be obtained.

Combination Vegetables and Noodles

A quick yet nourishing meal for your family. The combination of vegetables and noodles delicately flavoured with oyster sauce, chicken stock and sherry is simply delicious. Serve with sliced barbecued pork if desired.

PREPARATION TIME: *30 minutes*
COOKING TIME: *15 minutes*
SERVES 4–6

200 g thin fresh egg noodles
1/3 cup oil
3 eggs, lightly beaten
1 teaspoon sesame oil
1 tablespoon thinly shredded ginger
2 sticks celery, thinly sliced
200 g broccoli, chopped
1 cup shredded bok choi
1 cup shredded Chinese cabbage
1/2 cup chicken stock
2 teaspoons soy sauce
2 teaspoons oyster sauce
2 teaspoons dry sherry
1/2 teaspoon sugar
2 tablespoons toasted almonds

1 Cook noodles in large pan of boiling water until just tender; drain. Heat 2 tablespoons oil in wok or pan, add noodles, toss over high heat 2 minutes, remove from pan. Wipe pan dry.
2 Heat 1 teaspoon of oil in wok or pan. Add eggs, swirl over base of pan to make thin omelette. Cook without stirring or turning for 2 minutes over medium heat. Remove from pan, roll omelette up tightly and cut into thin shreds. Wipe pan dry.
3 Heat remaining oil and sesame oil in same pan. Add ginger, celery, broccoli, bok choi and cabbage, toss over high heat 1 minute.
4 Add combined stock, sauces, sherry and sugar to pan, stir over high heat 1 minute. Add noodles and egg, toss over medium heat for 2 minutes or until noodles are well coated and heated through. Serve sprinkled with toasted almonds.

Egg noodles are made from wheat flour and eggs, very similar to pasta. They are light golden to deep yellow in colour, and vary in thickness from thin vermicelli-like strands to thick, flat, fettucine-like lengths. They are sold fresh in plastic packets from Asian shops or dried in small bundles from supermarkets and specialty Asian stores. They can be served soft in stir-fries and should be boiled until just tender, drained well and added at the last minute to heat through. For crisp egg noodles, soak them briefly in hot water, drain well on absorbent paper and cook in a small amount of oil.

Above: Combination Vegetables and Noodles; Below: Egg Noodle and Roasted Capsicum Salad

Noodle, Mushroom and Broccoli Pie

A highly nutritious vegetable pie best eaten warm. The sweet and slightly chilli filling is best mellowed by the noodle base and the light and creamy potato topping.

PREPARATION TIME: *55 minutes*
COOKING TIME: *45 minutes*
SERVES 6

❈❈❈

2 tablespoons butter
200 g *button mushrooms, cut into quarters*
1 *red capsicum, seeded, chopped*
1 tablespoon *Hoi Sin sauce*
3 tablespoons *chilli sauce*
1 tablespoon *tomato sauce*
1 tablespoon *plain flour*
1/2 *cup water*
310 g *can butter beans, rinsed, drained*
125 g *broccoli, small florets*
125 g *Chinese wheat noodles*
1 *egg, lightly beaten*
2 *large potatoes, peeled, chopped into 2-cm cubes*
1/4 *cup butter*
1/4 *cup milk*

Asian wheat noodles are made of wheat flour and may be made with or without eggs. They are sold dried, fresh or wet. The wet or Hokkien wheat noodles are parboiled and either boiled again or fried and tossed with the other ingredients. Wheat noodles are made thick, thin, flat and round but always long as a sign of longevity.

1 Heat butter in pan. Add mushrooms, cook over medium heat for about 10 minutes or until browned. Add pepper, cook 5 minutes.
2 Blend sauces, and flour to a smooth paste. Add paste and water to pan, stir over medium heat until mixture boils and thickens.
3 Stir in beans and broccoli; remove from heat, cool.
4 Cook noodles in pan of boiling water until just tender; drain. When cool, combine noodles with egg. Spread and press noodle mixture over base of well greased 23-cm pie plate. Pour mushroom mixture onto noodle base, smooth surface.
5 Cook potatoes in small pan of boiling salted water until just tender; drain, mash with a fork. Add butter and milk, blend until smooth and creamy. Spoon potato mixture over mushroom filling, smooth surface. Bake pie in moderate oven 45 minutes. Stand 5 minutes before serving.

Spread and press noodle mixture over the base of a well greased 23-cm pie plate.

Spoon vegetable filling onto noodle base, smooth filling over the base.

Spoon potato mixture over vegetable filling, smooth top.

Noodle, Mushroom and Broccoli Pie

Noodle Filled Eggplant

A simple yet interesting combination of noodles and eggplant makes an ideal entrée, snack or lunch. Dried wheat noodles are available in supermarkets and specialty Asian shops.

PREPARATION TIME: *1 hour*
COOKING TIME: *10 minutes*
SERVES 4

1 tablespoon olive oil
2 large eggplants, halved lengthways
2 cups chicken stock
125 g dried wheat noodles
1 tablespoon lemon juice
2 tablespoons olive oil, extra
1 tablespoon chopped flat-leaved parsley
2 cloves garlic, crushed
½ teaspoon cracked black peppercorns
125 g Romano cheese, coarsely grated

1 Brush eggplant all over with oil. Place onto a foil-lined and greased oven tray, cut side down. Bake in moderate oven 1 hour, turning eggplant cut side up halfway through cooking time.
2 Bring stock to boil in small pan, add noodles. Reduce heat, simmer until noodles are tender. Cool noodles in stock; drain.
3 Scoop the soft flesh from the eggplant out into a bowl, leaving a 1–cm thick shell. Mash flesh with lemon juice, oil, parsley, garlic and peppercorns. Stir until smooth. Mix in noodles.
4 Spoon noodle mixture into eggplant shell, sprinkle with cheese. Bake in moderate oven 10 minutes or until eggplant has heated through and cheese has melted.
Note: If Romano cheese is unavailable, you may use Cheddar cheese as a substitute. For a tastier filling for the eggplant, you may wish to add ½ cup grated cheese through the filling before baking.

Noodles with Spinach Sauce

A quick and easy sauce that requires minimal preparation and fuss, and the results are delightful. Serve spinach sauce with fresh noodles of your choice.

PREPARATION TIME: *5 minutes*
COOKING TIME: *15 minutes*
SERVES 4

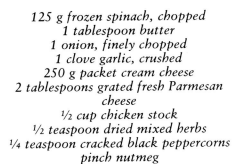

125 g frozen spinach, chopped
1 tablespoon butter
1 onion, finely chopped
1 clove garlic, crushed
250 g packet cream cheese
2 tablespoons grated fresh Parmesan cheese
½ cup chicken stock
½ teaspoon dried mixed herbs
¼ teaspoon cracked black peppercorns
pinch nutmeg
375 g flat noodles

1 Heat spinach in pan over low heat 5 minutes or until almost all liquid is absorbed; remove from pan, keep warm.
2 Heat butter in same pan. Add onion, stir over low heat 5 minutes or until onion is soft.
3 Blend or process spinach, onion, garlic, cream cheese, Parmesan, stock, herbs, peppercorns and nutmeg until almost smooth. Return mixture to pan, bring to boil, reduce heat, simmer uncovered 5 minutes.
4 Cook noodles in large pan of simmering water until just tender; drain. Add noodles to sauce, stir over low heat until well coated and heated through. Serve sprinkled with chopped fresh herbs or fresh grated Parmesan cheese, if desired.

Noodles with Spinach Sauce

Noodles in some shape or form are eaten every day by the peoples of China. The Chinese noodlemaker applies a skill that has been practised for over 1500 years. In the hands of a skilled noodlemaker, the lengths of the noodles remain unbroken, this is seen as a symbol of long life.

Egg Noodles with Cream Onion Sauce

An exceptional sauce that will make any meal complete. This sauce coats the egg noodles beautifully. Recipe is best made close to serving time.

PREPARATION TIME: *5 minutes*
COOKING TIME: *20 minutes*
SERVES 4

1 tablespoon butter
1 onion, chopped
1 cup cream
3 spring onions, finely chopped
1 teaspoon dried green peppercorns
½ teaspoon dried tarragon leaves
2 teaspoons cornflour
1 tablespoon milk
1 tablespoon horseradish cream
⅓ cup grated Parmesan cheese
375 g thick fresh egg noodles
1 tablespoon pine nuts, toasted
(optional)

1 Heat butter in pan. Add onion, cook over low heat 10 minutes or until well browned. Add cream, spring onions, peppercorns and tarragon leaves to pan. Bring to boil, reduce heat to low, simmer covered, 6 minutes.
2 Blend cornflour with milk, add sauce, stir until mixture boils and thickens.
3 Remove from heat, add horseradish cream and cheese, stir until sauce is smooth.
4 Cook noodles in large pan of boiling water until just tender; drain. Add noodles to sauce and toss over low heat until well coated and heated through. Serve noodles spinkled with pine nuts and chopped fresh parsley, if desired.
Note: Not suitable to freeze or microwave. Any fresh or dried egg noodles or long pasta strands would be enhanced by this rich creamy sauce.

Noodles in Black Bean Sauce

We often find black bean sauce associated with meat, poultry and seafood dishes. We have successfully adapted this popular sauce to flavour thick fresh egg noodles. You will find dried black beans in any Asian specialty shop.

PREPARATION TIME: *15 minutes*
COOKING TIME: *10 minutes*
SERVES 4

375 g thin fresh egg noodles
1 tablespoon oil
1 teaspoon sesame oil
1 tablespoon chopped fresh ginger
1 tablespoon crushed garlic
1 tablespoon dried black beans, finely chopped
¾ cup chicken stock
1 tablespoon Hoi Sin sauce
230 g can sliced bamboo shoots, drained
3 spring onions, sliced

1 Cook noodles in large pan of boiling water until just tender; drain.
2 Heat oils in wok or pan. Add ginger and garlic, stir over low heat 2 minutes; add beans. Stir 2 minutes.
3 Add chicken stock and Hoi Sin sauce to pan, bring to boil, boil 1 minute. Stir in noodles, toss until coated. Add bamboo shoots and spring onions, stir until heated through and ingredients are well combined. Serve immediately.

Noodles with Vegetable and Herbs

The delicately flavoured tomato sauce with red wine and herbs makes this a perfect meal for the family.

PREPARATION TIME: *20 minutes*
COOKING TIME: *25 minutes*
SERVES 4–6

Fresh egg noodles have a short shelf life. They should be kept sealed and refrigerated at all times until ready to be used. Do not purchase fresh noodles too far in advance nor in large quantities as they deteriorate quickly.

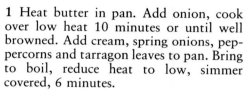

When a recipe requires noodles or pasta to be cut to required length, it is best to use a sharp pair of kitchen scissors to do so. Quite often it is easier and less messy to do so after it has been cooked.

1 tablespoon butter
1 tablespoon oil
1 onion, cut into strips
1 small red chilli, seeded, cut into strips
1 stick celery, sliced
1 carrot, sliced diagonally
1 tablespoon Taco seasoning mix
2 tomatoes, peeled and sliced
2 tablespoons tomato paste
½ cup red wine
1 bay leaf
½ cup beef stock
2 teaspoons chopped fresh basil
2 teaspoons chopped fresh parsley
375 g thin fresh rice noodles

1 Heat butter and oil in pan. Add onion, chilli, celery and carrot, cook over medium heat 5 minutes.
2 Add seasoning mix, tomatoes, paste, wine, bay leaf and stock to pan, bring to boil. Reduce heat to low, simmer covered, 15 minutes, stirring occasionally.
3 Add herbs to sauce, stir until combined.
4 Cook noodles in large pan of boiling water until just tender; drain. Serve noodles with sauce spooned over, and sprinkle liberally with grated cheese, if desired.
Note: Any herbs can be used with this combination of vegetables and tomatoes. Try, Rosemary, thyme or dried oregano.

Left: Noodles with Vegetables and Herbs; Right: Noodles in Black Bean Sauce

NOODLE VARIETIES

A large variety of fresh and dried noodles can be found. They can be made of wheat flour with or without eggs, these are sold as thin or thick, flat or rounded. They range in colour from light golden to deep yellow and are available fresh or dried. Other types are made of rice flour, these are sold as rice sticks or ribbons and rice vermicelli. There are also noodles made from soya or mung bean starch, called cellophane or bean thread noodles. Somen noodles are Japanese in origin and are made from ground buckwheat and wheat flour, they are beige coloured and some are subtly flavoured with Japanese green tea. Noodle shapes do not vary as much as pasta shapes. They may be thick, thin, flat or rounded but they will always be long, as they are a sign of longevity.

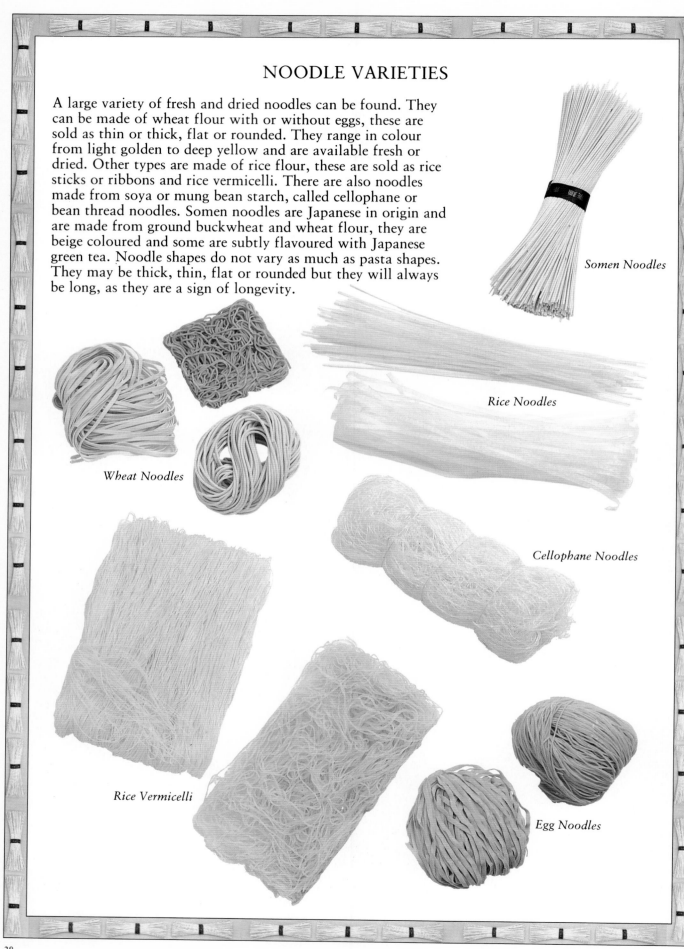

Somen Noodles

Rice Noodles

Wheat Noodles

Cellophane Noodles

Rice Vermicelli

Egg Noodles

Wonton Wrappers

Fresh Egg Noodles

Gow Gee Wrappers

Fresh Wheat Noodles

Fresh Rice Noodles

Pasta with Succulent Seafood

SUCCULENT FISH and shellfish combine with pasta in this special collection with superb results. We teamed the shorter pasta shapes, like penne and rigatoni, with chunky fish and seafood, this enables the moist seafood pieces to be trapped in and around the short pasta. The longer pasta types are best with creamy or tomato based seafood sauces.

Among pasta first courses elegant possibilities include Risoni and Creamy Cod Soup or Crabmeat Ravioli with Creamy Tomato Sauce. Options for main courses include a provincial style Seafood Ragout with Herbed Penne and Baked Pasta with Fish and Asparagus. Serve these or any of the pasta and seafood dishes with a fresh salad of seasonal greens and some crusty breads and you will have a magnificent meal for family and friends.

Above: Seafood Ragout with Herbed Penne (page 45); Below: Prawn and Olive Cannelloni (page 44)

Hearty Seafood and Pasta Soup

You will need about half the base quantity of fresh pasta for this recipe. Use our basic pasta dough recipe on page 56 and follow the techniques for rolling pasta on page 58. Gow gee or egg noodle wrappers may be used in place of fresh pasta. Put the soup together just before serving, the final results are fabulous. The flavours, colours and varying textures in this soup, complement each other beautifully.

PREPARATION TIME: *20 minutes plus 30 minutes pasta making*
COOKING TIME: *15 minutes*
SERVES 6

1 thick slice white bread, crusts removed
250 g white boneless fish fillet
1 teaspoon dried thyme leaves
24, 5–cm square pasta squares
6 cups fish stock
1 small leek, finely chopped
1 carrot, cut into fine strips 4–cm long
12 uncooked medium prawns, shelled, deveined
1 tablespoon oyster sauce

1 Blend or process bread and fish together until almost smooth; add thyme, stir until combined. Place a teaspoonful of mixture onto centre of each pasta square; moisten outer edge of square. Gather pasta up and around filling. Pinch edges together to enclose filling, and to resemble small pouches.
2 Bring stock to boil in pan, add leek and carrot. Reduce heat, simmer covered, 10 minutes. Add filled pasta, prawns and oyster sauce to stock, simmer uncovered, 5 minutes. Serve immediately.

Risoni and Creamy Cod Soup

The most essential ingredient in this recipe is the smoked cod, which gives the soup a most unique flavour and colour. The cod is soaked in water to extract some of the salt; little flavour is lost during this process.

To remove the vein from prawns without cutting with a knife simply place a sharp skewer into the centre of the prawn just under the vein and lift gently, the vein will follow.

PREPARATION TIME: *20 minutes plus 10 minutes standing time*
COOKING TIME: *30 minutes*
SERVES 4–6

250 g smoked cod, scaled and bones removed
1 tablespoon butter
1 onion, finely chopped
1 tablespoon plain flour
1 L water
pinch of saffron
pinch of nutmeg
½ cup risoni pasta
1 tablespoon lemon juice
2 spring onions
1 tablespoon chopped chives
½ cup cream
1 egg yolk

1 Cut cod into 2–cm pieces. Place in bowl, cover with boiling water; soak 10 minutes. Drain cod well.
2 Heat butter in pan. Add onion, cook over low heat 5 minutes. Add fish and flour to pan, toss until well coated. Stir over medium heat 2 minutes. Add water, saffron and nutmeg. Bring to boil, stir in risoni. Reduce heat, simmer uncovered, 20 minutes stirring occasionally.
3 Add lemon juice, spring onions and chives. Stir in combined cream and egg yolk. Remove from heat, serve immediately.
Note: Do not boil soup once cream and egg yolk have been added, as mixture may curdle.

Penne and Mixed Seafood Soup

A delicately flavoured soup comprising baby clams, calamari and mussels, with a hint of tomato and thyme. The soup is made complete with the addition of penne or other small pasta of your choice.

PREPARATION TIME: *5 minutes*
COOKING TIME: *25 minutes*
SERVES 4

2 rashers bacon, chopped
1 red capsicum, chopped

4 cups chicken stock
2 tablespoons tomato paste
1/4 teaspoon dried thyme leaves
125 g small penne pasta
290 g can baby clams, undrained
1 small calamari tube, cut into thin rings
500 g mussels in shells, scrubbed and
beards removed
Parmesan cheese (optional)

1 Cook bacon in pan over medium heat, 5 minutes or until well browned. Add pepper to pan, stir over heat **5** minutes or until soft.

2 Add stock, paste and thyme to pan. Bring to boil, add pasta. Simmer uncovered 10 minutes or until pasta is almost cooked, stir occasionally.

3 Add undrained clams, calamari and mussels. Simmer uncovered **5** minutes. Serve soup sprinkled with coarsely grated Parmesan cheese if desired.

Note: Unopened mussels must be discarded; they may not be safe to eat.

Above: Risoni and Creamy Cod Soup; Below: Hearty Seafood and Pasta Soup

Fettucine with Prawns and Mustard Sauce

The home-made fettucine in this recipe is beautifully dressed with the creamy prawn and mustard sauce. You may use fresh tagliatelle or spaghetti to replace the fettucine if desired; the results will be as good.

PREPARATION TIME: *25 minutes plus 30 minutes standing time*
COOKING TIME: *18 minutes*
SERVES 6

PASTA DOUGH
2½ cups plain flour
pinch salt
4 eggs, lightly beaten
1 egg for glazing, lightly beaten
SAUCE
2 tablespoons butter
2 tablespoons plain flour
¾ cup chicken stock
¼ cup red wine
1 cup cream
2 teaspoons mustard powder
1 teaspoon brown mustard seeds
750 g medium green prawns, shelled
2 tablespoons chopped fresh garlic chives

1 To make pasta dough: sift flour and salt into a bowl. Make a well in the centre and add the beaten eggs, gradually incorporate into flour with a fork. Turn onto a lightly floured surface and knead until smooth and elastic, about 5 minutes. Cover and stand for 30 minutes.
2 Divide pasta dough into four portions. Cover with a tea-towel. Roll one portion of pasta dough to 3–mm thickness, using rolling pin or pasta machine or sharp knife. Roll up the sheet of pasta completely, cut pasta into 5–mm wide strips. Carefully unroll strands. Repeat process with remaining portions of dough. Spread fettucine onto dry tea-towel, sprinkle with plain flour; set aside.
3 Heat butter in pan. Add flour, stir over medium heat 1 minute. Gradually stir in stock and wine, blend until smooth. Bring to boil, reduce heat, stir in cream, mustard powder and seeds, simmer uncovered 10 minutes.
4 Stir in prawns, simmer further 5 minutes or until prawns are tender. Remove from heat, stir in chives; cover, keep warm.

5 Shake excess flour from fettucine. Cook fettucine in large pan of boiling water for about 4 minutes or until just tender; drain. Serve with prawn and mustard sauce.

Prawn and Olive Cannelloni

Fresh lasagne sheets can be used to make larger cannelloni. Simply place the filling at the shorter end of the lasagne sheet, roll up and place seam side down in baking dish. Take care when removing baked cannelloni, use a flat slide for easier removal. Sauce is best made close to serving time.

PREPARATION TIME: *15 minutes*
COOKING TIME: *45 minutes*
SERVES 4

1 onion, chopped
2 slices thick bread, chopped
1 tablespoon chopped flat-leaved parsley
375 g green medium prawns, shelled, deveined, finely chopped
½ cup halved stuffed Spanish olives
1 tablespoon tomato paste
1 egg, lightly beaten
12 pre-cooked cannelloni shells
⅔ cup water
SPINACH CREAM
250 g packet frozen spinach, chopped
½ cup sour cream
2 tablespoons grated Parmesan cheese
2 teaspoons chopped fresh basil
2 teaspoons chopped fresh parsley

1 Blend or process onion, bread and parsley together until finely chopped.
2 Combine onion mixture with the prawns, olives, paste and egg in a bowl; stir until mixed.
3 Spoon prawn mixture into cannelloni tubes. Arrange filled tubes in single layer, side by side in greased, shallow ovenproof dish. Pour water over cannelloni. Cover with foil, bake in moderate oven 35 minutes or until tender.
4 Serve cannelloni with spinach cream.
5 To make spinach cream: heat spinach in pan over low heat 10 minutes or until thawed and all liquid has evaporated. Add cream, Parmesan and herbs. Stir until just heated through. Do not boil as sauce may separate.

Pasta machines are easily available, you really only need a simple pasta rolling machine with a few cutting attachments to achieve authentic results. After using your pasta machine clean it with a clean, dry cloth to remove any pasta or flour, never wash the pasta machine.

Olives are the fruit of the olive tree. Green olives are picked before they ripen. Black olives are allowed to fully ripen before they are picked. Neither olive can be eaten fresh from the trees as they have an extremely bitter flavour.

Seafood Ragout with Herbed Penne

The combination of seafood in a creamy sauce served over pasta flavoured with fresh herbs makes a hearty winter main or luncheon meal. All fish prawns or scallops or any combination of these could be used in this recipe.

PREPARATION TIME: *35 minutes*
COOKING TIME: *6 minutes*
SERVES 4–6

1 cup fish stock
1 cup dry white wine
1 leek, chopped
5 white peppercorns
2 bay leaves
350 g penne
150 mL cream
2 teaspoons cornflour
500 g white fish fillets, cut into 4–cm pieces
250 g large green prawns, peeled and deveined
250 g scallops, row intact
1 tablespoon chopped thyme
1 tablespoon chopped fresh dill
1 tablespoon chopped fresh parsley
30 g butter
shredded lemon and lime rind

1 Combine fish stock, wine, leek, peppercorns and bay leaves in a pan bring to the boil, reduce heat. Simmer uncovered for 15 minutes.
2 While stock is simmering, cook penne in pan of boiling water until just tender. Strain stock, return to pan.
3 Blend cream and cornflour, add to stock stir over gentle heat until mixture boils and thickens.
4 Add fish to cream sauce, cook 3 minutes. Add prawns and scallops, cook further 3 minutes. Drain penne, add herbs and butter, toss to combine until butter has melted. Place onto large serving dish or individual plates, top with seafood ragout. Garnish with lemon and lime shreds.

Risoni Seafood Soup

This is the soup for lovers of red wine and seafood. Seafood mix is available from your local fish monger. Any seafood of your choice could be used, try small prawns, mussels and crabmeat.

PREPARATION TIME: *20 minutes*
COOKING TIME: *13 minutes*
SERVES 4–6

¼ cup olive oil
1 onion, chopped
2 cloves garlic, crushed
2 tablespoons chopped parsley
1 cup red wine
1 cup tomato purée
2 cups water
2 tablespoons tomato paste
¾ cup risoni
300 g seafood mix
freshly ground black pepper
1 small Vienna loaf, sliced thinly
⅓ cup olive oil
extra 2 cloves garlic, crushed

1 Heat oil in large pan, add onion and garlic, cook until golden, add parsley and wine, cook for 5 minutes. Add tomato purée, water and tomato paste bringing to the boil, sprinkle in risoni and gently boil until risoni is just tender.
2 Stir in seafood mix, cooking for 3 minutes. Serve accompanied by crispy slices of baked Vienna loaf.
3 Prepare bread by placing slices of bread onto baking slide, brushing each slice with combined oil and garlic. Bake at 200°C until crisp and golden brown.

Basil can be kept covered in olive oil and used when making tomato based sauces. Simply snip leaves from stem, place in glass jar, pack down tightly and cover with oil. A bonus of this storage method is basil flavoured oil to use in your favourite salad dressing.

Risoni Seafood Soup

Salmon Filled Pasta Shells

Serve the filled pasta shells warm with the cold tomato and onion salad, and you will find that the two complement each other superbly.

PREPARATION TIME: *30 minutes plus 20 minutes standing time*
COOKING TIME: *12 minutes*
SERVES 4

12 extra large pasta shells
¼ cup risoni shaped pasta
100 g thinly sliced smoked salmon, finely chopped
1 small onion, finely chopped
½ red capsicum, finely chopped
1 tablespoon sour cream
1 teaspoon finely chopped fresh dill
TOMATO AND ONION SALAD
2 large tomatoes, finely chopped
1 onion, finely chopped
1 tablespoon lemon juice
¼ teaspoon cracked black peppercorns
2 teaspoons finely chopped fresh dill

1 Cook pasta shells in large pan of boiling water until just tender; drain. Cook risoni in pan of boiling water until just tender; drain, cool.
2 Combine risoni with salmon, onion, capsicum, sour cream and dill; mix well.
3 Spoon filling into prepared shells. Place filled shells onto foil-lined and greased oven tray. Bake in moderate oven 12 minutes or until shells are just heated through. Serve risoni and salmon shells with tomato onion salad.
4 To make tomato and onion salad: combine all ingredients in a bowl; stand covered, 20 minutes.

Spiral Pasta with Mussels and Herbs

A superb idea to consider next time you are entertaining. Add the mussels, herbs and pasta just before serving. The herb flavoured cream sauce will coat the mussels and pasta beautifully. You may use spiral pasta, small penne pasta shells for this recipe.

PREPARATION TIME: *30 minutes*
COOKING TIME: *10 minutes*
SERVES 6

375 g spiral pasta
1 kg mussels in shells
2 tablespoons butter
1 onion, chopped
1 small leek, cut into fine 10–cm strips
200 g button mushrooms, sliced
²/₃ cup cream
2 teaspoons tomato paste
2 tablespoons dry white wine
2 tablespons lemon juice
1 tablespoon chopped flat-leaved parsley
1 tablespoon finely chopped basil
1 tablespoon chopped garlic chives
1 red chilli, seeded, cut into thin strips

1 Cook pasta in large pan of boiling water until just tender; drain. Scrub mussels under cold water; remove beards.
2 Heat butter in pan. Add onion, leek and mushrooms, stir over medium heat for about 5 minutes or until onion and leek are soft.
3 Add cream, paste, wine and juice, bring to boil. Add mussels, bring to boil, reduce heat, simmer covered for about 3 minutes or until shells have opened. Discard unopened shells.
4 Add herbs, chilli and pasta to pan, stir until combined and just heated through.

Pasta should only be rinsed in cold water if it is to be served cold or used in a baked pasta dish. Pasta should never be rinsed in hot water this only cooks the pasta further, causing sticking as it cools. When pasta is cooked to your liking, drain well in a colander, return to pan or warmed serving bowl, add a little olive oil and or a couple of tablespoons of sauce and toss well, serve immediately.

Salmon Filled Pasta Shells

Above: Fettucine and Prawns with Mustard Sauce (page 44); Below: Spiral Pasta with Mussels and Herbs

Crabmeat Ravioli with Creamy Tomato Sauce

Canned, fresh or frozen crabmeat can be used for this recipe.

PREPARATION TIME: *35 minutes plus 30 minutes standing time*
COOKING TIME: *10 minutes*
SERVES 4–6

RAVIOLI DOUGH
2½ cups plain flour
4 large eggs
1 egg, lightly beaten
CRAB FILLING
300 g crabmeat
2 tablespoons soft butter
¼ cup chopped fresh basil
TOMATO SAUCE
500 mL cream
¾ cup white wine
¾ cup water
1 onion, cut in half
1 tablespoon butter
1 tablespoon flour
3 tomatoes, peeled, seeded and chopped

1 To make ravioli dough: see Basic Pasta Dough page 56.
2 Prepare filling while pasta is standing. Combine crabmeat, butter and basil.
3 For sauce: place cream, white wine, water and onion in a pan. Bring to the boil, then reduce to a simmer. Simmer gently until mixture is reduced by half. Melt butter in pan, add flour, mix well and cook 1 minute. Remove from heat, gradually stir in reduced cream mixture. Return to heat stirring constantly until mixture boils and thickens. Add tomatoes, simmer for 5 minutes.
4 Roll out half the pasta dough very thinly into a rectangle. Roll out remaining pasta dough to a rectangle slightly bigger than the first. On the first rectangle place teaspoonfuls of filling at 5–cm intervals in straight rows. Brush the dough between the filling with egg. Place the second sheet of dough carefully over the top. Press down before cutting to seal sheets of dough together. Use a floured crimped pastry wheel to cut into squares.
5 Drop ravioli into a large pan of boiling water. Cook until just tender. Drain. Combine with sauce. Serve.

Every city or town in Italy has its own trademark pasta. The region of Tuscany is famous for lasagne, tagliatelle and tortellini. Farfalle or bow shaped pasta originated from Northern Italy. Fettucine is regarded as the pasta most typical of Rome.

Gradually incorporate eggs into flour with a fork or your hand if this is easier.

Combine crabmeat, butter. and chopped basil for the filling.

Ravioli can be filled by hand (see page 97) or with an attachment from pasta machine.

The attachment for ravioli makes filling, sealing and cutting very easy.

Fettucine and Tuna with Capers

Canned tuna has been used for this recipe, fresh cooked tuna could be easily substituted. Capers add a certain piquancy to this dish. Any ribbon pasta could be used in place of fettucine.

PREPARATION TIME: *10 minutes*
COOKING TIME: *5 minutes*
SERVES 4–6

500 g spinach and plain fettucine
¼ cup olive oil

2 cloves garlic, crushed
225 g can tuna, drained
⅓ cup lemon juice
60 g butter
2 tablespoons chopped capers
½ teaspoon chopped chilli
lemon slices, for garnish
extra 1 tablespoon capers, for garnish

1 Place fettucine in pan of boiling water cook until just tender.
2 Heat oil in pan, add garlic, cook 1 minute add tuna cook 2 minutes longer. Add lemon juice, butter, capers and chilli, stir into tuna and cook on low until heated through.
3 Drain fettucine, add to sauce mix gently to combine. Place onto serving plate, top with lemon slices and capers.

Left: Fettucine with Tuna and Capers; Right: Crabmeat Ravioli with Creamy Tomato Sauce

For optimum flavour and texture seafood is best eaten on the day of purchase. Seafood can be kept in the refrigerator for 2 to 3 days if stored correctly, to do so remove from plastic bags, place into a glass dish and cover with paper and then aluminium foil.

The golden rule to observe when purchasing fish is make sure it is fresh, look for these signs; pleasant sea smell, bright unsunken eyes, glossy bright skin, bright red gills, firm flesh that springs back when touched and the flesh should not appear water logged.

Farfalle Pasta with Oysters and Scallops

Tender shellfish cooked in tomato sauce with the added tang of orange juice and rind. This recipe can also be served chilled. Spiral pasta can be used in place of bow.

PREPARATION TIME: *12 minutes*
COOKING TIME: *10 minutes*
SERVES 4–6

¼ cup olive oil
2 cloves garlic, crushed
250 g drained bottled oysters
250 g scallops
½ cup roughly chopped basil
500 g tomatoes, peeled, seeded and chopped
juice and rind of 1 orange
freshly ground black pepper
500 g farfalle (bow) pasta
extra ⅓ cup shredded orange rind
extra 1 tablespoon olive oil

1 Heat oil in pan, add oysters and scallops, cook 2 minutes. Remove, set aside. Add basil, tomatoes, orange juice and rind. Stir to combine. Simmer 10 minutes.
2 Add pasta to large pan of boiling water, cook until just tender. Add oysters and scallops to sauce, simmer 5 minutes.
3 Drain pasta, add shredded rind and oil, toss to combine. Place onto large serving platter. Top with sauce. Serve immediately.

Baked Pasta with Fish and Asparagus

Rigatoni has been used in this baked pasta dish, macaroni or penne could be substituted. Be careful not to overcook fish initially otherwise it will dry out in the oven.

PREPARATION TIME: *20 minutes*
COOKING TIME: *15 minutes*
SERVES 4–6

350 g rigatoni
1 bundle fresh asparagus, trimmed and cooked
250 g white fleshed fish fillets
juice ½ lemon
4 white peppercorns
250 g ricotta cheese
3 eggs, lightly beaten
125 g freshly grated Parmesan cheese
lemon, for garnish

1 Cook rigatoni in boiling water until just tender. Drain and set aside.
2 Place fish, lemon juice and peppercorns into shallow pan, add enough water to just cover. Cook fish over gentle heat for 5–6 minutes.
3 Place ⅓ rigatoni into well greased ovenproof dish. Add asparagus and fish, then add half remaining rigatoni. Top with ricotta, place remaining rigatoni on top.
4 Combine eggs and Parmesan pour over top. Bake at 180°C for 15 minutes or until heated through. Garnish with lemon and serve.
Note: Asparagus can be cooked in large shallow pan of boiling water until just tender, taking approximately 8 minutes. Drain well on absorbent paper before using. Canned asparagus could be used.

Fish, Prawn and Anchovy Lasagne

A slightly unusual version of the more renowned lasagne. The combination of seafood, beans, tomatoes, sweet chilli sauce and basil is absolutely delicious. The addition of mozzarella makes it a little more traditional, while it mellows down the stronger seafood flavours.

PREPARATION TIME: *35 minutes*
COOKING TIME: *40 minutes plus 5 minutes standing time*
SERVES 6

250 g boneless fish fillet, cut into 1–cm cubes
375 g green medium prawns, shelled, deveined, chopped finely
410 g can tomatoes, crushed
1 tablespoon Thai sweet chilli sauce

310 g can red kidney beans, rinsed, drained
45 g can anchovy fillets, drained, chopped
1 tablespoon finely chopped fresh basil
240 g packet pre-cooked lasagne sheets
375 g mozzarella cheese, grated

1 Combine fish, prawns, tomatoes, chilli sauce, beans, anchovies and basil in a large bowl.
2 Spoon small amount of mixture over base of greased ovenproof lasagne dish. Cover with a layer of lasagne sheets; sprinkle with mozzarella cheese.
3 Divide seafood mixture into three portions. Spread one portion over cheese layer, top with lasagne sheets; sprinkle with cheese. Repeat layering process, ending with cheese on top. Cover lasagne with foil. Bake in moderate oven 30 minutes. Remove foil. Bake further 10 minutes. Stand 5 minutes before serving. Serve lasagne with a tossed salad and herb bread.

Left: Fish, Prawn and Anchovy Lasagne; Right: Farfalle Pasta with Oysters and Scallops

Spaghetti with Mussels and Tomato Sauce

What could be more satisfying, spaghetti and mussels in a tomato wine sauce. Mussels must be cleaned thoroughly before cooking. Scrub each mussel with a stiff nylon brush and rinse them several times in clean cold water.

PREPARATION TIME: *25 minutes*
COOKING TIME: *15 minutes*
SERVES 4–6

¼ *cup olive oil*
2 cloves garlic, crushed
1 small red chilli, chopped
1 × 425 g can tomatoes
150 mL white wine
1 kg mussels, scrubbed
500 g spaghetti
parsley sprigs, for garnish

1 Heat oil in large pan, add garlic and chilli cook for 2 minutes. Add tomatoes and wine, bring to the boil then reduce to a simmer and add mussels and cook for 8–10 minutes.
2 Cook spaghetti in boiling water until just tender. Drain.
3 Add spaghetti to tomato mixture, mix to combine. Place into large serving bowl garnish with parsley sprigs.
Note: After cooking discard any unopened mussels.

Spaghetti with Mussels and Tomato Sauce

Tagliatelle and Tuna Slice

Tagliatelle and tuna slice can be served hot or cold. It is great for picnics, lunches and barbecues. Try spaghetti or small penne pasta as a substitute for tagliatelle in this recipe. Sauce can be made a day ahead if desired.

PREPARATION TIME: *20 minutes*
COOKING TIME: *30 minutes*
SERVES 4–6

125 g dried tagliatelle
425 g tuna in brine, drained, flaked
1 red capsicum, finely chopped
340 g can asparagus spears, drained, chopped
2 spring onions, chopped
1 cup grated Cheddar cheese
4 eggs, lightly beaten
SAUCE
¼ *cup cream*
¼ *cup mayonnaise*
1 tablespoon tomato paste
1 tablespoon prepared French dressing
2 teaspoons chopped chives

1 Cook tagliatelle in large pan of boiling water until just tender; drain.
2 Combine tuna, capsicum, asparagus, spring onions, cheese and tagliatelle in a bowl. Add eggs, stir until combined.
3 Press mixture into a well greased square ovenproof dish. Bake in a moderate oven 30 minutes or until golden. Stand 5 minutes before cutting. Serve with cocktail sauce.
4 To make sauce: blend all ingredients together in a bowl.

Spiral Pasta and Fish Salad

Any firm white fleshed fish can be used for this recipe.

PREPARATION TIME: *30 minutes*
COOKING TIME: *nil*
SERVES 4–6

250 g spiral pasta, cooked and cooled
250 g whole fish or fillets, cooked and cooled
2 small white onions, finely sliced
2 small ripe tomatoes, quartered
12 black olives, stones removed
1 clove garlic, crushed
2 teaspoons French mustard
2 tablespoons white wine vinegar
1/3 cup olive oil
3 hard-boiled eggs, quartered

1 Combine pasta, fish (skin and bones removed), onions, tomatoes and olives. Place into large serving bowl.
2 Mix together garlic, mustard, vinegar and olive oil. Pour over pasta mixture. Top with hard-boiled eggs.
Note: Hard-boiled eggs should be placed into cold water immediately after cooking to prevent grey ring forming on yolk.

Warm Seafood and Pasta Salad

A salad of warm seafood, cold pasta and crisp salad flavoured with vermouth and vinaigrette. This makes an excellent start to a formal meal. Spiral pasta can be used in place of penne.

PREPARATION TIME: *10 minutes*
COOKING TIME: *4 minutes*
SERVES 4–6

1/2 cup water
1/2 cup white wine
2 spring onions, chopped
24 scallops, row intact
3 calamari, cleaned and cut into 1–cm pieces
1 tablespoon oil
24 green prawns, peeled and deveined
1/2 cup vermouth
300 g penne pasta, cooked, drained and cooled
1/2 bunch watercress, washed and diced
1 butter lettuce, washed, dried and torn into pieces
extra 1/4 cup oil
1/4 cup white wine vinegar
freshly ground black pepper
1 1/2 bunch chives, cut into 5–cm lengths

1 Place water, white wine and spring onions into large shallow pan bring to simmering point. Add scallops and cook for 1 minute remove, add calamari rings cooking 1 minute further, remove. Discard cooking liquid.
2 Add oil to pan, heat. Add prawns, cook 1 minute. Pour in vermouth and return scallops and calamari. Cook 1 minute, remove from heat.
3 Combine pasta, watercress, lettuce, oil, vinegar and pepper toss gently to combine. Place onto large serving plate, add seafood, garnish with chives.
Note: Choose watercress with dark green leaves and use as soon as possible after purchase.

Pasta can be coated with small amount of olive oil to prevent it sticking together. For extra flavour try some of the herbed flavoured oils.

Warm Seafood and Pasta Salad

Spaghetti with Chunky Fish and Tomato Sauce

A quick and economical dish to prepare when in a hurry, using a jar of bottled spaghetti sauce as the base. Sauce is best served over spaghetti, tagliatelle or fettucine.

PREPARATION TIME: *5 minutes*
COOKING TIME: *10 minutes*
SERVES 4

2 tablespoons oil
1 onion, chopped
1 stick celery, chopped
1 green capsicum, chopped
250 mL bottled, prepared spaghetti sauce
250 g boneless fish fillet, cut into 2–cm cubes
½ teaspoon dried oregano leaves
¼ teaspoon cracked black peppercorns
500 g spaghetti

1 Heat oil in pan. Add onion, celery and capsicum, cook over medium heat 5 minutes.
2 Add sauce to pan, stir gently until mixture boils. Add fish, oregano and peppercorns. Simmer covered, 5 minutes.
3 Cook spaghetti in large pan of boiling water until just tender; drain. Serve chunky fish sauce spooned over spaghetti, sprinkled with grated cheese and small oregano leaves.

Spaghetti and Chunky Fish and Tomato Sauce

Penne and Fish with Fruity Almond Sauce

This recipe is suitable to serve as the main course of a formal meal. In place of raisins, dried apricots could be used and rigatoni in place of penne.

PREPARATION TIME: *20 minutes*
COOKING TIME: *10 minutes*
SERVES 6

90 g butter
500 g white fish fillets, cut into strips
2 tablespoons plain flour
1 small onion, finely chopped
1 cup white wine
100 g raisins
50 g slivered almonds
1 tablespoon lemon juice
2 teaspoons honey
400 g penne
2 egg yolks
50 g toasted flaked almonds, for garnish

1 Melt 60 g butter in a large pan, add fish, cook gently until tender. Set aside and keep warm.
2 Add remaining butter to pan, add onion cook until soft. Remove from heat and stir in flour, gradually add wine return to heat stir until mixture boils and thickens. Add raisins, almonds, lemon juice and honey. Simmer gently for 15 minutes.
3 While sauce is simmering: cook penne in boiling water until just tender. Drain and transfer to heated serving dish. Place fish over penne. Keep warm. Remove sauce from heat, stir a little of the sauce into egg yolks, whisk into sauce. Return to the heat, heat gently 2–3 minutes. Pour over penne and fish, garnish with almonds.

Note: After returning combined sauce and egg yolks to heat, stir constantly over a low heat until warm to prevent egg yolks separating.

Above: Penne and Fish with Fruity Almond Sauce; Below: Baked Pasta with Fish and Asparagus (page 50)

MAKING PASTA AT HOME

Fresh home-made pasta is decidedly an enjoyable eating experience. Once a few basic techniques are familiar, and with a little patience and practice, pasta making will become an extremely easy and enjoyable task.

BASIC PASTA DOUGH

Generally home-made pasta is made from flour and eggs. For the very best results start with the freshest ingredients — good quality plain flour and fresh eggs. To make enough pasta for 6 people as a main course you will need:

2½ cups plain flour
4 large eggs, lightly beaten

1 Sift flour into a bowl or onto a clean work surface, use a fork to make a well in the centre. Add the eggs.

2 Gradually incorporate the flour and the eggs, using the fork. Continue to mix the flour and egg mixture with your hand if this is easier.

3 When the mixture begins to form a ball, turn onto a lightly floured surface and knead the mixture for about 3 minutes. The dough should begin to be smooth and elastic, continue kneading for about 10 minutes. Discard any crusty bits of dough as you knead, these will cause the pasta strands to break. The dough should have a supple velvety consistency.

4 Cover the dough with a clean cloth and allow to stand for 30 minutes.

Note: Pasta dough can be made in a food processor, simply combine flour and egg and process until mixture forms a smooth ball. Knead mixture as above.

Sift flour onto work surface, break the eggs directly into centre of flour mound.

Gradually incorporate the flour and eggs using a fork or your hand if this is easier.

As mixture begins to form a ball, turn onto a lightly floured surface and knead for 3 minutes.

Knead dough until smooth and elastic, continue kneading for about 10 minutes.

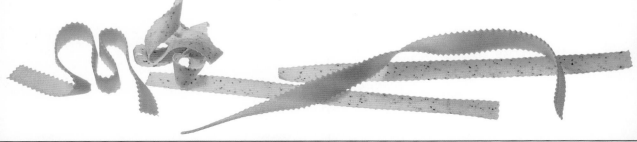

PASTA DOUGH VARIATIONS

You can add texture and variety to home-made pasta by adding simple flavourings. Possibilities are almost limitless. Try the addition of chilli, paprika, freshly cracked black pepper or nutmeg.

Simply incorporate any of these with the sifted flour, use about 1 to 1½ teaspoons of any of these spices. You can add 2 teaspoons of freshly grated lemon rind or 1 tablespoon tomato paste and crushed garlic or 2 tablespoons finely chopped fresh herbs (such as basil or rosemary) to the beaten eggs. Make dough as for plain pasta dough. Spinach flavoured pasta is very well liked, we found the best results were obtained by combining 2/3 cup of spinach purée with 1 large egg and incorporating this mixture with the flour; make as for plain pasta.

For spinach flavoured pasta, combine flour, 2/3 cup spinach purée and 1 large egg.

Gradually incorporate the flour, spinach and egg with a fork or your hand if this is easier.

Knead dough on a lightly floured surface until dough is of a supple, velvety consistency.

For pepper or spiced pasta simply add about 1½ teaspoons of pepper or ground spice to eggs.

After kneading, rest and roll dough as for plain pasta, cut, pepper or spice pasta as desired.

Here we cut pepper pasta into pappedelle and then farfalle shapes using a serrated cutter.

TECHNIQUES FOR ROLLING PASTA BY HAND

To roll pasta by hand you need a long flat work area and a long rolling pin. There is also a great need to work quickly so that the pasta does not dry out and crack.

1 Lightly flour the work surface, press the dough flat. Start from the centre using the rolling pin to roll dough forward then backward, repeat this motion until the dough has stretched to an even thickness.

2 As you roll keep lifting the sheet of pasta and turning it 45 degrees. When you roll lift the far edge of the rolling pin as you push forward to stretch the dough.

3 The sheet of pasta will become quite large, allow 1/3 of the dough to hang over the edge of work bench as you continue to turn and roll.

4 The pasta should be smooth and fine and of an even colour, darker areas indicate thickness. It will take time and practice to hand roll pasta as thinly as machine rolled pasta, don't be discouraged if you don't have absolute success the first time.

5 For lasagna or any filled pasta use the rolled pasta immediately. For pasta strands: allow the pasta to dry, by placing over a clean cloth or hang in an airy place over a broom handle suspended between two chairs. As a general rule, let the pasta dry for about 15 minutes, it must be dry enough to prevent sticking but not so dry that it begins to become brittle.

6 After drying, the dough is ready to cut into any length or shape required. Roll up the sheet of pasta completely, use a sharp flat-bladed knife to cut pasta into 5-mm wide strips. Carefully unroll the strands to their full length and allow the strands to dry over a clean cloth. Pasta can also be wound loosely into small nest-like shapes, place on a clean cloth. When all the pasta has been cut it is then ready to cook.

Note: Pasta can also be allowed to dry completely (this may take up to 24 hours) and stored in airtight containers in a dry cupboard for up to 2 months. Take care when handling the dried pasta as it will be quite brittle.

To roll dough: start from the centre using a rolling pin to roll dough backward and forward.

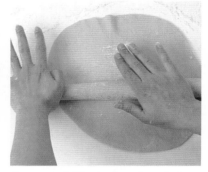
As you roll lift the far edge of the rolling pin as you push forward to stretch the dough.

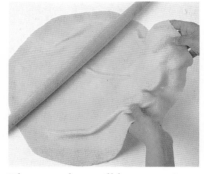
The pasta sheet will become quite large, it should be smooth and fine and of an even colour.

For lasagne, or any filled pasta like ravioli, cut and use the pasta sheet immediately.

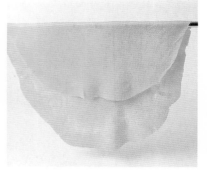
To make pasta strands like fettucine, allow the pasta to dry in airy place for about 15 minutes.

To make fettucine, roll up the pasta sheet with a sharp flat-bladed knife to cut pasta into 5-mm strips.

TECHNIQUES FOR ROLLING PASTA BY MACHINE

There are many pasta machines available for home use they can be very simple hand cranking machines or electric machines which mix the dough and extrude it through a cutter of your choice. Unless you intend to make tremendous amounts of fresh pasta a simple pasta rolling machine would certainly suffice, these pasta machines roll the dough into thin sheets and have several cutting attachments that allow you to cut pasta into the shapes and widths you desire.

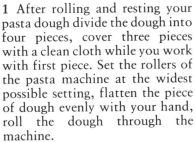

1 After rolling and resting your pasta dough divide the dough into four pieces, cover three pieces with a clean cloth while you work with first piece. Set the rollers of the pasta machine at the widest possible setting, flatten the piece of dough evenly with your hand, roll the dough through the machine.

2 Continue rolling the dough through the machine. Fold the dough in half to fit through rollers until it is smooth and supple.

3 When the pasta is smooth, set the rollers a groove closer, roll the pasta through, keep setting the rollers closer until pasta is the desired thickness.

4 The pasta will now be quite long, lay the pasta sheet on a clean cloth or place the pasta sheet over a broom stick suspended between two chairs. As a general rule let the pasta dry for about 15 minutes, it must be dry enough to prevent sticking but not so dry that it begins to become brittle. Repeat rolling with the remaining dough pieces as the first piece dries.

5 After drying, the dough is ready to cut into any length or shape required. A final rolling for lasagna and larger pieces of pasta dough for cutting ravioli and tortellini is needed.

6 Pass the sheets of dough through the machine with the selected cutter, do not stop cranking the machine until the entire sheet has been fed through to avoid breaking the pasta strands.

Note: Allow the strands to dry over a clean cloth. Pasta can also be wound loosely into small nest-like shapes, place them on a clean tea-towel to dry. To cook: pick the pasta up with the tea-towel holding the four corners and let the pasta slide into the boiling water.

Set pasta rolling machine at widest setting, cut dough into four equal pieces, roll through machine.

Roll dough until smooth and supple, set rollers a groove closer, continue to roll pasta sheet.

Pass pasta through machine at desired thickness, crank machine until entire sheet runs through.

Noodles with Succulent Seafood

T HIS COLLECTION IS Asian inspired, we've teamed egg noodles, rice noodles, wontons and cellophane noodles with the best from the east. Coconut cream, sesame oil, garlic, ginger and chillies all feature with moist, rich seafood in these flavoursome recipes.

Throughout Asia noodles are eaten day and night, as snacks and meals in restaurants, at home and at food stalls.

Expand your own culinary horizons at home with Crisp Prawn and Crabmeat Wontons, Noodle and Coconut Fish Soup or Noodle and Prawn Salad with Peanut Sauce and the impressive Chilli Crab and Soft Noodles.

Crisp Prawn and Crabmeat Wontons (page 64), Chilli Crab and Soft Noodles (page 64)

Noodle and Coconut Fish Soup

A spectacular combination of flavours come together beautifully to make this soup complete. The coconut milk, lime juice, chilli and coriander are just a few of the ingredients that contribute to this soup's exceptional flavour.

PREPARATION TIME: *10 minutes*
COOKING TIME: *15 minutes*
SERVES *4*

4 cups chicken or fish stock
½ cup coconut milk
1 small red chilli, seeded, finely chopped
2 teaspoons fish sauce
2 tablespoons lime juice
1 spring onion, finely chopped
100 g thin dried egg noodle bundles
250 g white boneless fish fillet, cut into 1–cm cubes
1 tablespoon finely chopped coriander

1 Combine stock, coconut milk and chilli together in a pan, bring to boil. Add fish sauce, lime juice and spring onion, stir until combined. Reduce heat and simmer 5 minutes.
2 Add noodles, simmer uncovered. Add fish, simmer uncovered 5 minutes or until fish and noodles are just tender.
3 Stir in coriander, serve immediately.

Coriander is the herb used extensively in Asian and Middle Eastern cuisine. All of the herb is used — the soft green foliage, the stems and the white root section. Coriander should never be finely chopped. The root section should be scrapped before chopping. Coriander is best wrapped in aluminium foil and stored in the vegetable crisper. Rinse in cold water just before using.

Vermicelli, Corn and Crabmeat Soup

Rice vermicelli are often used in small quantites, particularly in soups, as they swell and double in size once they absorb liquid during cooking. They have very little flavour, but add an interesting texture to the consistency of this subtle crab flavoured soup.

PREPARATION TIME: *5 minutes*
COOKING TIME: *20 minutes*
SERVES *4*

2 tablespoons butter
100 g button mushrooms, sliced thinly
2 tablespoons plain flour
3 cups chicken stock
170 g can flaked crabmeat
50 g vermicelli, cut into 10–cm lengths
310 g can creamed corn
1 tablespoon soy sauce
2 spring onions, finely chopped

1 Heat butter in pan. Add mushrooms, cook over medium heat 5 minutes or until golden. Add flour, cook 2 minutes, stirring constantly.
2 Add stock to pan, blend until smooth. Bring mixture to boil. Add crabmeat, noodles and corn, stir until combined. Reduce heat, simmer covered 10 minutes or until noodles are just tender.
3 Stir in soy sauce and spring onions. Serve soup immediately.

Noodles with Oysters and Scallops

Paper thin slices of fresh peeled ginger gives this recipe its distinctive flavour.

PREPARATION TIME: *10 minutes*
COOKING TIME: *4–5 minutes*
SERVES *4–6*

300 g fresh egg noodles
1 tablespoon oil
1 × 5–cm piece of fresh ginger, sliced thinly
300 g fresh scallops
250 g bottled fresh oysters, drained
¾ cup chicken stock
2 tablespoons oyster sauce
2 teaspoons cornflour
2 tablespoons water

1 Place noodles in a large pan of boiling water, cook until just tender.
2 Heat oil in large shallow pan or wok. Add ginger, scallops and oysters stir-fry for 3–4 minutes, remove. Add stock, oyster sauce and blended cornflour and water, stir until mixture boils and thickens, return seafood, heat 1 minute.
3 Drain noodles place onto large serving plate spoon over scallops, oysters and ginger sauce. Serve immediately.

Above: Noodle and Coconut Fish Soup; Below: Noodles with Oysters and Scallops 63

Crisp Prawn and Crabmeat Wontons

Filling ideas for wonton wrappers are endless, this prawn and crab filling is simple to prepare and a delight to eat. Treat your family and friends to these light and crisp nibbles any time.

PREPARATION TIME: *25 minutes*
COOKING TIME: *5 minutes*
SERVES 6

375 g green medium prawns, shelled,
deveined, finely chopped
1 cup flaked crabmeat
2 cloves garlic, crushed
¼ teaspoon ground ginger
2 teaspoons chopped fresh mint
½ cup bean sprouts
40 wonton wrappers
oil, for deep frying
DIPPING SAUCE
2 tablespoons lemon juice
1 tablespoon Hoi Sin sauce
1 tablespoon Thai sweet chilli sauce

1 Combine prawns, crab, garlic, ginger, mint and sprouts in bowl.
2 Place 1 teaspoonful of mixture into centre of wrappers. Brush each corner lightly with water. Carefully bring corners up and over filling to meet in centre, forming a square parcel. Press ends together firmly.
3 Deep-fry wontons a few at a time until crisp and golden; drain on absorbent paper. Serve prawn and crab wontons with dipping sauce.
4 To make dipping sauce: combine all ingredients together in a bowl.

Chilli Crab and Soft Noodles

Use fresh crabmeat pieces for this recipe, or any fresh frozen or canned crab.

PREPARATION TIME: *20 minutes*
COOKING TIME: *7–10 minutes*
SERVES 4–6

2 tablespoons oil
200 g egg noodles, cooked and cooled
2 teaspoons grated ginger
1 clove garlic, chopped
200 g crabmeat pieces
1 bunch asparagus, cut into 4–cm
lengths, cooked
1 cup bamboo shoots
1 red capsicum,
thinly sliced into strips
1 tablespoon oil
2 tablespoons soy sauce
1 teaspoon chilli sauce
10–12 large Chinese cabbage leaves

1 Plunge cabbage leaves one at a time into boiling water for 30 seconds, remove place into iced water. Remove, dry in clean tea-towel.
2 Heat oil in large pan, add noodles and cook 3–4 minutes remove and set aside. Remove oil from pan, add ginger, garlic and crabmeat stir 2–3 minutes. Remove, add to noodles.
3 Add asparagus, bamboo shoots and capsicum to noodle mixture. Combine oil, soy sauce and chilli, add to noodle mixture, toss well to combine.
4 Place cabbage leaves onto a large serving dish and crab and noodle mixture into serving bowl. Allow guests to fill and roll their own cabbage leaves. When serving offer Sweet Asian Chilli Sauce, if desired.
Note: Bamboo shoots are sold in cans whole or sliced. Store unused bamboo shoots in water and refrigerate for up to two days.

Seafood in a Noodle Basket

Noodle baskets can be served hot or cold. They can be prepared several days before required and stored in a airtight container. If desired, baskets can be reheated for 10 minutes in slow oven. This recipe is ideal to serve as an entrée.

PREPARATION TIME: *35 minutes*
COOKING TIME: *nil*
SERVES 4–6

200 g noodles, cooked, well drained
oil, for deep frying

Asian pasta or noodles are made of wheat flour, with or without eggs. These are sold as thin or thick flat and rounded noodles, they can be fresh or dried. Others are made from rice flour these are sold as rice sticks or rice vermicelli. There are also noodles made from soya or mung bean starch, they are sold as cellophane or bean thread noodles, they need to be soaked in water to soften before using. Wontons and gow gee wrappers are also classed as Asian noodles.

250 g cooked prawns
250 g scallops, poached and cooled
1 tablespoon shredded preserved red
ginger
1/3 cup rice vinegar
1 tablespoon sugar
3 teaspoons soy sauce
dark outer leaves of lettuce, finely
shredded
extra shredded red ginger, for garnish

1 Lay noodles between absorbent paper pat dry. Place enough noodles to cover inside of a small metal strainer. Press the noodles in place with a second strainer. Lower carefully into deep hot oil, cook until golden brown. Remove from oil, carefully separate strainers. Turn stainer upside down, gently tap base to remove noodles, drain well on absorbent paper.
2 Combine prawns and scallops with ginger, vinegar, sugar and soy sauce. Spoon mixture evenly into noodle baskets.
3 Place shredded lettuce onto large serving platter or individual plates, sit filled noodle baskets on top. Garnish with extra shredded red ginger.
Note: Preserved red ginger is available in jars or packets from Asian specialty shops. Rice wine vinegar is a Japanese vinegar if unavailable use white wine vinegar.

Seafood Noodle Hot Pot

An Asian flavoured seafood soup that could be served as part of a meal or a meal on its own. Seafood is added at the very last so as not to overcook and become tough. Any combination of seafood could be used in this recipe.

PREPARATION TIME: *15 minutes*
COOKING TIME: *14 minutes*
SERVES 4–6

2 tablespoons vegetable oil
4–cm piece fresh ginger, peeled and
grated
4 spring onions, trimmed and sliced
1/2 small cabbage, shredded
8 cups water or fish stock
1/4 cup soy sauce
2 tablespoons dry sherry

1 teaspoon sesame oil
200 g flat rice noodles
250 g bottled oysters, drained
250 g scallops
250 g green prawns, peeled and deveined,
tail intact
shredded green tops of spring onion, for
garnish

Seafood Noodle Hot Pot

1 Heat oil in large pan, add ginger, onions and cabbage, cook gently until cabbage is just soft.
2 Add water, soy sauce, sherry and sesame oil bring to the boil, add noodles cook 8 minutes. Reduce to a simmer, add prepared seafood and cook for 3–4 minutes or until prawns are just cooked.
3 Place into serving bowl, top with shredded spring onion.

Layered Noodle and Salmon

Ricotta cheese is made from the whey leftover from cheese such as provolone, pecorino and mozzarella. It is usually very white in colour, smooth in texture and bland in flavour. Ricotta is often combined with stronger flavoured ingredients for both sweet and savoury dishes.

A simple dish the whole family will enjoy. Serve it hot or cold, cut into wedges accompanied with a crisp green salad.

PREPARATION TIME: *10 minutes*
COOKING TIME: *35 minutes*
SERVES 4–5

250 g dried wheat flour noodles
210 g *can red salmon, undrained, bones removed*
1 tomato, peeled and finely chopped
2 teaspoons finely chopped fresh dill
1 tablespoon lemon juice
1 cup finely chopped broccoli
2 eggs, lightly beaten
200 g ricotta cheese, sieved
3 spring onions, finely chopped
2/3 cup grated Cheddar cheese

1 Cook noodles in large pan of boiling water until just tender; drain, cool.
2 Mash salmon in bowl with fork. Add tomato, dill, lemon juice and broccoli; mix well.
3 Combine noodles with eggs, ricotta and spring onions until well coated.
4 Press half noodle mixture over base of paper lined and greased 20–cm springform pan. Press salmon mixture over noodles, smooth over with back of spoon. Top with remaining noodle mixture. Sprinkle with grated cheese, bake in moderate oven 35 minutes or until golden. Stand 5 minutes before serving.

Layered Noodle and Salmon

Eggplant, Tomato and Prawns with Noodles

The combination of eggplant, zucchini and fresh tomatoes with thyme together with the prawns, garlic, lemon juice and noodles is absolutely exquisite.

PREPARATION TIME: *10 minutes plus 20 minutes standing time*
COOKING TIME: *15 minutes*
SERVES 4

2 teaspoons salt
1 large eggplant, cut into thick 6–cm long strips
3 tablespoons olive oil
2 small zucchini, cut into thin 6–cm long strips
3 large tomatoes, peeled and sliced
2 tablespoons lemon juice
1/2 teaspoon sugar
1/2 teaspoon thyme leaves
1/2 teaspoon cracked black peppercorns
375 g medium uncooked prawns, shelled, deveined
3 cloves garlic, crushed
250 g fresh thick noodles

1 Sprinkle salt over eggplant in colander, toss lightly; stand over sink 20 minutes. Rinse eggplant under cold running water; drain well.
2 Heat oil in pan. Add eggplant and zucchini, stir over a medium heat 5 minutes or until vegetables are soft. Add tomatoes, lemon juice, sugar, thyme and peppercorns, simmer uncovered 5 minutes, stirring occasionally.
3 Add prawns and garlic to pan, stir over low heat 3 minutes or until prawns are just cooked.
4 Cook noodles in large pan of boiling water until tender; drain. Stir noodles into sauce, toss until combined. Serve sprinkled with extra thyme leaves if desired.
Note: Sauce may be served over noodles if preferred.

Above: Eggplant, Tomato and Prawns with Noodles; Below: Combination Noodle with Fish and Cucumber Braise

Prawn and Noodle Omelette with Sweet and Sour Sauce

Bean thread noodles, or vermicelli, can be purchased in most supermarkets or Asian specialty shops. Cook omelettes in a lightly but well oiled omelette or crêpe pan.

PREPARATION TIME: *20 minutes plus 30 minutes standing time*
COOKING TIME: *20 minutes*
SERVES 6

50 g bean thread noodles, covered with water for 30 minutes
10 eggs
250 g small cooked prawns
4 spring onions, finely chopped
oil, for frying
SAUCE
1 tablespoon oil
2 teaspoons grated ginger
½ red capsicum, cut into thin strips
½ green capsicum, cut into thin strips
½ small cucumber, cut in half, seeded, cut into thin strips
⅓ cup pineapple juice
⅔ cup water
2 tablespoons tomato sauce
2 teaspoons brown vinegar
1 teaspoon brown sugar
2 teaspoons cornflour, blended with 2 tablespoons water

1 Place noodles in pan of boiling water cook for 5 minutes, drain well and cut into 5-cm pieces.
2 Beat eggs until well combined, add prawns, spring onions and noodles, mix well to combine. Heat a small amount oil in small frying pan adding ½ cup measure of egg mixture. Cook gently until mixture is firm. Turn and cook other side. Place onto heated serving plate. Continue in same manner until all mixture has been used.
3 Prepare sauce while cooking omelettes. Heat oil in small pan, add ginger, cook 1 minute. Add capsicum and cucumber strips cook 3–4 minutes. Add pineapple juice, water, tomato sauce, vinegar, brown sugar and blended cornflour. Stir constantly until mixture boils and thickens.
4 Serve omelettes stacked on large on individual serving plates and pour the sauce over.

Left: Prawn and Noodle Omelette with Sweet and Sour Sauce; Right: Marinated Octopus and Noodle Salad

Marinated Octopus and Noodle Salad

Marinated octopus, grilled or barbecued, is served hot over cold noodles. Choose the smallest octopus available as these are the most tender. Octopus can also be chilled before serving and covered with a little extra olive oil to prevent them becoming dry.

PREPARATION TIME: *30 minutes plus overnight marinating*
COOKING TIME: *nil*
SERVES 4–6

1 kg baby octopus
½ cup olive oil
½ cup soy sauce
½ cup mango chutney
1 tablespoon lime juice
2 cloves garlic, crushed
1 small lime, sliced, each cut into four
1 red chilli, cut into very thin strips
1 bunch coriander, roughly chopped
2 tablespoons teriyaki sauce
300 g wheat noodles, cooked and cooled
1 mango, peeled and sliced

1 To prepare octopus: remove heads by cutting just below eyes, remove beak and rinse under cold water. Place octopus into large glass basin. Combine soy sauce, chutney, juice and garlic, pour over octopus, mix well until octopus is well coated in marinade. Cover and refrigerate several hours or overnight.
2 Remove octopus from marinade place under hot grill or on barbecue plate and cook until tender brushing with marinade during cooking.
3 Combine lime, chilli, coriander and teriyaki pour over noodles, toss to combine. Place onto large serving platter, top with octopus and garnish with mango slices.

Seafood Wontons with Garlic Sauce

Wonton wrappers can be filled and then deep fried, boiled or steamed.

PREPARATION TIME: *20 minutes*

COOKING TIME: *15–20 minutes*
SERVES 4–6

375 g white fish, fillets boned and minced
125 g flaked crabmeat
¼ cup chopped chives
1 tablespoon lime juice
48 wonton wrappers
1 egg, lightly beaten
oil, for deep frying
SAUCE
1 teaspoon vegetable oil
2 cloves garlic, crushed
½ cup lime marmalade
⅓ cup soy sauce
3 tablespoons lime juice
¼ cup water
extra chives, for garnish

1 Combine fish, crabmeat, chives and lime juice.
2 Cut each wonton into 6–cm round. Spread 24 rounds onto large wooden board, place a spoonful of filling into centre of each round. Brush edge with beaten egg, top with remaining rounds. Press down edges to seal.
3 Heat oil in large pan. Deep-fry a few at a time until golden brown, drain on absorbent paper. Transfer to heated serving platter.
4 Prepare sauce while frying ravioli. Heat oil in small pan, add garlic, cook 1 minute, add marmalade, soy and lime juice and water stir well to combine. Bring to the boil remove from heat. Serve separately or over ravioli. Garnish with extra chives.

Soy sauce is a salty brown sauce produced from the natural fermentation of soya beans. It is used extensively in all Asian cookery. Chinese soy is available in dark or light, either can be used when a recipe just calls for soy sauce.

Seafood Wontons with Garlic Sauce

Combination Noodle with Fish and Cucumber Braise

Cellophane and egg noodles are combined together in soy vinegar sauce. Topped with fish and crunchy cucumber. Choose firm white fleshed fish, free from skin and bone.

PREPARATION TIME: *30 minutes plus 10 minutes soaking time*
COOKING TIME: *8 minutes*
SERVES 4–6

2 tablespoons vegetable oil
2 cloves garlic, finely sliced
100 g cellophane noodles, soaked in water to soften
100 g fine egg noodles, soaked in water to soften
2 tablespoons soy sauce
2 tablespoons malt vinegar
1 small red chilli, cut into fine shreds
1 tablespoon vegetable oil
1 teaspoon sesame oil
2 cucumbers, peeled, seeded and sliced
500 g white fish fillets, cut into serving size pieces
2 teaspoons dry sherry
2 teaspoons soy sauce
1 teaspoon cornflour
1/3 cup water
1 tablespoon toasted sesame seeds

1 Heat oil in large pan or wok, add garlic cook until golden brown. Add well drained noodles cook 3–4 minutes. Pour in combined soy, vinegar and chilli, toss gently. Set aside and keep warm.
2 Heat oils in large pan, add cucumber stir-fry quickly 2–3 minutes, remove set aside. Add fish pieces cook quickly 2–3 minutes or until cooked through. Remove set aside.
3 Add combined sherry, soy, cornflour and water to pan cook on low heat until mixture boils and thickens. Return noodles, cucumber and fish to pan toss gently until heated through.
4 Place on serving plate, sprinkle with sesame seeds. Serve immediately.
Note: Toast sesame seeds in a moderate oven for about 3 minutes.

Cellophane noodles are made from mung bean starch, they are thin, glossy and translucent, and sold dried in small, tied bundles. They are generally added to soups and wet dishes as they absorb other flavours well. Soak them in hot water for about 10 minutes or until soft, drain on absorbent paper before adding to stir-fries. They do not need soaking before adding to soups.

Add noodles to wok, stir-fry, pour in combined soy, vinegar and chillies.

Add fish pieces to wok, stir-fry gently for about 2–3 minutes or until just cooked.

Add combined sherry, soy, cornflour and water to wok; add noodles.

Return fish and cucumber to wok, toss together with noodles and sauce.

Egg Noodles with Anchovy and Caper Sauce

This light and smooth sauce is made complete with the addition of capers, parsley and lemon juice. For a more subtle anchovy flavour, soak the drained anchovies in milk for about 20 minutes. Drain and use as directed.

PREPARATION TIME: *15 minutes*
COOKING TIME: *10 minutes*
SERVES 4

1 tablespoon butter
1 onion, chopped
45 g can anchovy fillets in oil, drained
1 tablespoon flour
1 cup chicken stock
1 tablespoon small capers, rinsed and drained
2 teaspoons finely chopped parsley
2 teaspoons lemon juice
375 g fresh egg noodles

1 Heat butter in pan. Add onion, cook over medium heat 5 minutes or until onion is well browned. Add anchovies, stir over low heat 1 minute.
2 Add flour to pan, cook over low heat 2 minutes. Gradually add stock, blend until smooth. Bring mixture to boil, boil 1 minute.
3 Remove from heat; cool slightly. Blend or process sauce until smooth. Return sauce to pan. Add capers, parsley and lemon juice. Stir over low heat until just warm through.
4 Cook noodles in large pan of simmering water until tender; drain. Add noodles to sauce, stir until coated with sauce. Serve immediately.

Spicy Calamari filled Noodle Nests

The noodles require no cooking prior to deep-frying. Follow our step-by-step guide to Perfect Noodle Baskets on page 75.

PREPARATION TIME: *40 minutes*
COOKING TIME: *5 minutes*
SERVES 4

250 g thick fresh noodles
oil, for deep-frying
3 large calamari tubes, cut into 5–cm squares
1 tablespoon oil
3 cloves garlic, crushed
1 green capsicum, cut into 2–cm squares
2 tablespoons tomato sauce
1 tablespoon tomato paste
3 teaspoons Worcestershire sauce
¼ teaspoon Tabasco sauce
½ cup chicken stock
½ teaspoon cornflour

1 Divide noodles equally into four portions. Arrange one portion evenly over inside of lightly oiled strainer. Press top stainer onto noodles. Lower strainer into hot oil, deep-fry until noodles are browned; remove from oil, drain on absorbent paper. Carefully remove basket from strainer, repeat with remaining noodles.
2 Using a sharp knife, score calamari pieces diagonally in one direction then in the opposite direction to give a cross-hatched pattern.
3 Heat oil in wok or pan. Add garlic, pepper and calamari, toss over high heat 1 minute. Add combined remaining ingredients, stir until mixture boils and thickens. Spoon calamari mixture into noodle baskets.

Capers, olive green in colour, are the flower buds of a wild, climbing thorny plant. They have been used as a condiment in cooking for thousands of years. Capers grow wild in Cyprus, Sicily, North Africa and France. Capers are often salted and preserved in vinegar. They can be added to dishes such as soups, casseroles, pizzas and salads.

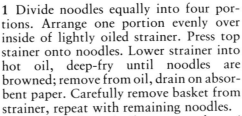

Spicy Calamari filled Noodle Nests

Noodle and Prawn Salad with Peanut Dressing

A refreshingly light and tasty salad that requires only minutes to prepare. The salad can be made a day ahead; pour dressing over just before serving.

PREPARATION TIME: *15 minutes*
COOKING TIME: *nil*
SERVES 4

250 g thick fresh egg noodles
1 large calamari tube, cut cross-hatched pieces
200 g broccoli, cut into small florets
100 g snow peas, trimmed
12 medium, cooked prawns, shelled and deveined
PEANUT DRESSING
¼ cup oil
2 tablespoons lime juice
1 tablespoon smooth peanut butter
2 tablespoon Hoi Sin sauce
¼ teaspoon garam masala

1 Cook noodles in large pan of boiling water until just tender; drain.
2 Drop calamari into small pan of simmering water, cook 1 minute or until tender; remove and drain. Boil, steam or microwave broccoli and snow peas until just tender, rinse under cold water; drain.
3 Combine noodles with seafood and vegetables in large bowl. Pour over dressing, toss until well coated.
4 To make peanut dressing: combine all ingredients in a jar, shake well.

Noodle and Prawn Salad with Peanut Dressing

Noodles with Garlic and Octopus

This richly flavoured sauce made with baby octopus, is served over fresh noodles. It is best served as a main course.

PREPARATION TIME: *20 minutes*
COOKING TIME: *1 hour*
SERVES 4–6

2 tablespoons olive oil
1 large onion, sliced
410 g can tomatoes, crushed
1 bay leaf
¼ teaspoon whole allspice
1 tablespoon brown vinegar
¼ cup dry red wine
1 cup beef stock
1 kg baby octopus, heads removed and discarded
375 g fine fresh noodles
3 cloves garlic, crushed
3 spring onions, chopped

1 Heat oil in pan. Add onion, cook over medium heat 1 minute. Add tomatoes, bay leaf, allspice, vinegar, wine and stock; bring to boil.
2 Add octopus to pan, simmer covered 40 minutes, stirring occasionally. Simmer uncovered further 20 minutes or until octopus is tender.
3 Meanwhile, cook noodles in large pan of boiling water until just tender; drain.
4 Stir garlic and spring onions into octopus sauce, stir over high heat 1 minute. Serve octopus sauce over noodles.

Note: To clean octopus use a small sharp knife and remove the gut by either cutting off the head entirely or by slitting open the head and removing the gut. Pick up the body and use the index finger to push beak up and remove. Discard. Wash octopus thoroughly. If sauce has not reduced sufficiently, thicken with cornflour mixed with a little water, add to sauce, simmer until mixture boils and thickens.

Above: Spicy Calamari filled Noodle Nests (page 71); Below: Noodles with Garlic Octopus

TECHNIQUES FOR FILLING AND SHAPING WONTON NOODLES

The most versatile noodle would seem to be wonton wrappers. These small noodle squares can be filled with many varied stuffings, they may be savoury or sweet. These paper thin squares, made of flour and egg, are available fresh or frozen from Asian specialty stores. Fresh wrappers can be made at home from a basic pasta dough, you will need to roll the dough out until it is almost transparent, cut the wrappers into 8–cm squares — they may also be cut with a sharp round or fluted cutter and used to make gow gee's. Commercial wonton noodles are best thawed slowly in the refrigerator; keep moist under a damp, clean tea-towel during use as they dry and crack easily. Savoury filled wontons may be steamed, deep-fried or added to soups, serve them with a soy and ginger dipping sauce. Sweet filled wontons are generally deep-fried and served dusted with icing sugar.

Prawn and Pork Wontons

Any mince may be used to fill wontons, try fish, chicken or veal.

PREPARATION TIME: *20 minutes*
COOKING TIME: *12 minutes*
MAKES *about 30*

1 tablespoon Chinese dried prawns
1 tablespoon chopped coriander
1 clove garlic
125 g cooked, peeled prawns
375 g minced pork
2 teaspoons soy sauce
1 egg
30 wonton wrappers
oil, for deep frying

1 Finely chop the dried prawns, coriander and garlic in a food processor, add fresh prawns, pork mince, soy sauce and egg; process until smooth.
2 Use a narrow pastry brush dipped in water to moisten a square 2–cm in from the edge of the wrapper.
3 Place a teaspoonful of mixture onto centre of each wrapper, gather the sides of the wrapper up

Use a pastry brush dipped in water to moisten a 2–cm edge around wonton wrapper.

Gather the edges up and around filling, pleating the edges together as you enclose filling.

and around filling; pleating the moistened edges together as you enclose filling. Carefully fan out the top of each completed wrapper.

4 Place wontons on lightly oiled paper in a bamboo steamer. Cover, cook over simmering water for about 10–12 minutes. Serve with soy dipping sauce.

TECHNIQUES FOR PERFECT NOODLE NESTS

Noodle baskets are used throughout Asia, notably China to present stir-fried dishes, particularly delectable seafood meals and special occasion dishes.

   To make perfect noodle nests every time follow our step-by-step instructions. Use fresh vegetable or peanut oil and always check the temperature of the oil before beginning to cook nests. Test with a small piece of bread; the bread should cook evenly to a light golden colour and rise to the top of the pan within about 30 seconds to 1 minute. Take care to lower the nests gently into the hot oil. Once the oil starts to bubble over the nests, tip the baskets slightly to check their colour, remove them from the oil as they begin to turn a light golden colour.

Noodle Nests

This quantity makes four nests, they can be made and deep-fried up to one day in advance, reheat in a moderate oven until warm.

PREPARATION TIME: *20 minutes*
COOKING TIME: *3 minutes*
MAKES 4

250 g thick fresh egg noodles
oil, for deep-frying

1 Divide noodles into four equal portions. Arrange one portion evenly over inside of a lightly oiled strainer.
2 Press a slightly smaller, oiled strainer onto the noodles, forming a basket shape.
3 Carefully lower strainers into moderately hot oil, hold strainers together as they cook, until noodles are golden brown; remove from oil.
4 Invert strainers over absorbent paper, carefully remove basket from strainer, repeat with remaining noodles.
Note: Nests can be frozen in a rigid container for up to a month. Reheat in a moderate oven or by briefly re-frying.

Arrange noodles evenly over the inside of a lightly oiled strainer.

Carefully lower strainers into moderately hot oil.

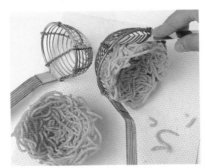

Invert strainer over absorbent paper, carefully remove noodle nest.

Pasta with Meat, Poultry & Game

DISCOVER CLASSICAL Italian regional pasta dishes in this chapter and be inspired by the new and innovative recipes we share with you. Among the collection you will find Oven Baked Lasagne made in true traditional fashion and simple Penne and Chilli Beef Bake, both perfect family style dishes. There are quick and easy recipes for Spaghetti with Prosciutto and a rich flavoursome Tagliatelle with Rosemary Quail Sauce, the pasta is dressed with the sauce and served as a first course and the quail is a moist, succulent second course. These and more await you.

Tagliatelle with Rosemary Quail Sauce (page 82)

Macaroni, Chicken and Asparagus Soup

You may use any small macaroni shape of your choice for this recipe. Soup is best made just before serving as it will thicken on standing.

PREPARATION TIME: *15 minutes*
COOKING TIME: *25 minutes*
SERVES 4

250 g chicken breast fillets, thinly sliced
2 tablespoons seasoned flour
60 g butter
1 medium onion, chopped
340 g can asparagus spears, undrained
3 cups rich chicken stock
½ teaspoon brown mustard seeds
1 cup small macaroni
2 tablespoons finely chopped flat-leaved parsley
2 tablespoons sour cream

1 Place chicken and flour in a bag, toss until chicken is well coated with flour.
2 Heat butter in pan. Add onion, cook over medium heat for 2 minutes or until onion is soft. Add chicken, stir until browned but not cooked through.
3 Add asparagus, stock and mustard seeds, bring to boil, reduce heat, simmer covered 5 minutes. Add macaroni to pan, simmer covered 10 minutes or until pasta is just tender, stirring occasionally.
4 Add parsley and sour cream, stir until just heated through.

Macaroni, Chicken and Asparagus Soup

Penne, Pea and Lamb Shank Soup

This soup, delicately flavoured with cumin seed, can be served with penne pasta, rigatoni or spiral shaped pasta. It is best made close to serving time and makes an ideal first course.

PREPARATION TIME: *15 minutes*
COOKING TIME: *1 hour 15 minutes*
SERVES 6

2 tablespoons olive oil
3 lamb shanks (about 1 kg), well trimmed of fat
2 medium onions, cut into strips
¼ cup dry red wine
½ teaspoon cracked black peppercorns
½ teaspoon cumin seeds
1 whole cinnamon stick
1 dried bay leaf
4 cups water
2 tablespoons soy sauce
2 tablespoons tomato paste
1 cup small penne pasta
1 cup fresh or frozen peas, thawed
1 cup fresh or frozen broad beans
1 clove garlic, crushed

1 Heat oil in pan. Add lamb, cook over high heat for about 3 minutes each side or until well browned. Remove from pan, drain on absorbent paper.
2 Add onions to pan, cook over medium heat for about 3 minutes or until well browned. Return lamb to pan, add wine, peppercorns, cumin, cinnamon, bay leaf and water; bring to boil. Reduce heat, simmer covered, 1 hour or until lamb is tender.
3 Remove lamb from pan, discard bay leaf and cinnamon stick from stock. Add soy sauce and tomato paste to pan, stir until combined. Bring to boil, add pasta, simmer covered, 5 minutes stirring occasionally.
4 Meanwhile, cut lamb into bite-size pieces; discard bones. Return lamb, peas and broad beans to pan, simmer covered, further 4–5 minutes or until pasta is just tender. Stir in garlic just before serving.
Note: It is essential to brown the meat and onions well before adding the wine to obtain the maximum colour and flavour required for this soup.

Fettucine and Lamb Salad with Thai Dressing

A refreshing light salad with a Thai influence. This salad can be made with fresh or dried fettucine or taglitelle or even large penne pasta. The combination flavours and colours make this salad ideal for entertaining.

PREPARATION TIME: *30 minutes plus 10 minutes standing time*
COOKING TIME: *nil*
SERVES 6

2 tablespoons oil
375 g lamb fillets, trim all fat
200 g dried fettucine
1 small cucumber, cut into thin 10–cm long ribbons
1 carrot, cut into thin 10–cm long ribbons
1 zucchini, cut into thin 10–cm long ribbons
1 Spanish red onion, cut into thin strips from top to base of onion
THAI DRESSING
2 tablespoons mint jelly
2 tablespoons finely chopped fresh coriander
2 teaspoons finely chopped red chilli
2 tablespoons olive oil
1/3 cup white wine vinegar

1 Heat oil in pan. Add lamb fillets, cook over high heat for 6 minutes or until well browned all over. Remove pan from heat, stand covered, 10 minutes.
2 Cook fettucine in large pan of boiling water until just tender, drain, rinse under cold water; drain.
3 Cut lamb into long thin strips, place into large bowl. Add fettucine and vegetables to bowl, toss together lightly. Pour half the dressing over salad, cover, refrigerate salad until ready to serve. Just before serving, transfer salad to a serving bowl and pour remaining dressing over.
4 To make dressing: pass mint jelly through a fine strainer into a small bowl. Whisk jelly, coriander, chilli, oil and vinegar until combined.

Pappardelle and Chicken Salad

Here's a great starter to any meal. Serve it at your next dinner party as an entrée or accompaniment to a main course. It not only looks impressive, it tastes great too. You may substitute pappardelle pasta with tagliatelle or fettucine if desired.

PREPARATION TIME: *20 minutes plus 1 hour standing time*
COOKING TIME: *nil*
SERVES 4

2 skinned chicken breast fillets, cut into 1–cm cubes
2 teaspoons soy sauce
1 teaspoon sambal oelek
1/4 teaspoon cracked black peppercorns
200 g pappardelle pasta, cut in half lengthways
1 tablespoon oil
1 small radicchio lettuce, torn into bite-sized pieces
1 cup (about 100 g) mustard cress
REDCURRANT AND ORANGE DRESSING
1 tablespoon redcurrant jelly, sieved
1 tablespoon red wine vinegar
1 tablespoon orange juice
1/2 teaspoon grated orange rind
2 teaspoons soy sauce
1/3 cup olive oil

1 Place chicken, soy sauce, sambal oelek and peppercorns in small bowl; mix well. Stand, covered, 1 hour.
2 Meanwhile cook pasta in large pan of boiling water until just tender; drain, allow to cool.
3 Heat oil in pan. Add chicken, cook over high heat 3 minutes or until well browned and cooked through. Remove from pan, cool.
4 Arrange radicchio leaves over base of serving plates. Pile mounds of pappardelle over radicchio. Scatter with chicken pieces and mustard cress. Pour dressing over just before serving.
5 To make dressing: whisk all ingredients together in a jug until combined.

When cooking pasta for salads, add about two cups of cold water to the pan of water just before you drain the pasta, this cools and prevents the pasta overcooking, drain and run the pasta under cool water, drain thoroughly, add a little oil to pasta before adding dressing. Pasta salads are best served slightly chilled or at room temperature.

Above: Fettucine and Lamb Salad with Thai Dressing (page 79); Below: Penne, Pea and Lamb Shank Soup (page 78)

Pepperoni and Shell Pasta Salad

You may use small shell pasta, small elbows or small penne pasta for this salad. The creamy dressing will not only coat the pasta beautifully, but will complement the hotness of the pepperoni sausage.

PREPARATION TIME: *20 minutes*
COOKING TIME: *nil*
SERVES 4–6

200 g small shell pasta
150 g thinly sliced pepperoni sausage
200 g button mushrooms, cut in half
½ red capsicum, chopped
½ green capsicum, chopped
½ cup pitted black olives, cut in half
DRESSING
¼ cup prepared bottled French dressing
1 tablespoon sour cream
2 teaspoons mayonnaise
1 tablespoon finely chopped flat-leaved parsley

1 Cook pasta in large pan of boiling water until just tender; drain. Rinse pasta under cold water and drain again.
2 Combine pepperoni, mushrooms, capsicum, olives and pasta in large bowl.
3 Add dressing, toss until all ingredients are well coated.
4 To make dressing: whisk French dressing, cream and mayonnaise together until smooth; stir in parsley.

Pepperoni and Shell Pasta Salad

¼ cup olive oil
375 g rump steak, finely chopped
3 cloves garlic, chopped
5 small red chillies
1 bay leaf
2 ripe tomatoes, peeled, chopped
½ cup chicken stock
2 tablespoons soy sauce
2 tablespoons finely chopped fresh basil
375 g large penne pasta
CHEESE TOPPING
2 tablespoons butter
2 tablespoons flour
2 cups milk
100 g Kefalograviera or pecorino cheese, coarsely grated
2 eggs, lightly beaten
¼ cup coarse fresh breadcrumbs

1 Heat oil in medium pan. Add beef, cook over high heat 5 minutes or until well browned. Add garlic, chillies, bay leaf, tomatoes, stock and soy sauce, bring to boil. Add basil, reduce heat and simmer uncovered, 20 minutes. Remove from heat, discard bay leaf.
2 Cook pasta in large pan of boiling water until just tender; drain. Combine pasta with chilli beef sauce, spoon into a deep greased ovenproof dish. Top with cheese sauce, sprinkle with breadcrumbs. Bake in moderate oven 30 minutes or until golden. Stand 5 minutes before serving.
3 To make cheese topping: heat butter in pan. Add flour for 1 minute on medium heat. Gradually blend in milk, stir until mixture is free of lumps, and sauce boils and thickens. Remove from heat, stir in cheese and eggs.

Kefalograviera cheese, also kown as *Kefalotyri* is used extensively in Greek cooking. It is a direct translation from the Greek word meaning head cheese. The cheese is pressed into moulds which consequently resemble the shape of either a skull or hat.

Penne and Chilli Beef Bake

This baked pasta dish is best made with large penne pasta, medium-sized rigatoni or large spirals. The pasta is deliciously flavoured with a light tomato sauce spiked with dried red chillies. Penne and chilli beef bake is ideal served as a main course with crisp green side salad.

PREPARATION TIME: *25 minutes*
COOKING TIME: *1 hour 10 minutes*
SERVES 4–6

Tagliatelle with Rosemary Quail Sauce

Sweet capsicum and rosemary quail sauce can be served with fresh or dried tagliatelle as a first course. The quails are removed from the sauce and served as part of the second course. Serve the quails with polenta wedges and a salad.

PREPARATION TIME: *10 minutes*
COOKING TIME: *40 minutes*
SERVES 4

2 tablespoons plain flour
1 teaspoon ground paprika
4 small quails, halved
¼ cup olive oil
2 red capsicums, finely chopped
1 large onion, finely chopped
410 g can tomatoes, undrained, crushed
1 teaspoon dried rosemary leaves
1 teaspoon brown sugar
¼ cup red wine
500 g tagliatelle

1 Place flour, paprika and quails into plastic bag. Toss until quails are well coated, shake off excess flour.
2 Heat 2 tablespoons of the oil in pan. Add quails, cook over medium heat 2 minutes each side or until golden but not cooked through. Remove from pan, drain on absorbent paper. Wipe pan dry.
3 Heat remaining oil in same pan. Add capsicum and onion, stir over low heat 2 minutes. Cover and cook for 10 minutes, stirring occasionally. Add tomatoes, rosemary, brown sugar and red wine, bring to the boil. Return quails to pan, stir into sauce. Reduce heat to low, simmer covered, 20 minutes or until quails are tender. Remove quails from sauce, keep warm.
4 Meanwhile, cook tagliatelle in large pan of boiling water until just tender, drain. Serve sauce over pasta.

Traditional Chicken Lasagne

A truly rich and aromatic lasagne with a chicken mince, giblet and liver filling and mozzarella cheese. Recipe can be made a day ahead; an ideal meal for entertaining.

PREPARATION TIME: *55 minutes*
COOKING TIME: *40 minutes*
SERVES 4–6

1 tablespoon olive oil
1 large onion, finely chopped
1 red capsicum, finely chopped
125 g pancetta, finely chopped
500 g lean chicken mince
250 g chicken giblets, finely chopped
200 g chicken livers, finely chopped
1 tablespoon brandy
1 cup rich chicken stock
2 tablespoons finely chopped flat-leaved parsley
2 teaspoons dried oregano leaves
2 cloves garlic, crushed
375 g mozzarella cheese, cut into thin slices
250 g packet pre-cooked lasagne sheets
½ cup cream

1 Heat oil in pan. Add onion, capsicum and pancetta, cook over medium heat 10 minutes or until browned. Add mince, giblets and livers, cook 10 minutes or until browned, stirring occasionally.
2 Add brandy to pan, stir well. Add stock, parsley and oregano, bring to boil. Reduce heat, simmer covered 20 minutes. Remove from heat, stir in garlic.
3 Spoon ¼ of filling over base of greased ovenproof dish. Top with a layer of lasagne sheets, and a layer of mozzarella slices. Repeat layering, ending with lasagne sheet on top. Reserve final layer of mozzarella cheese for later.
4 Pour cream evenly over lasagne. Cover with foil, bake in moderate oven 20 minutes. Remove foil. Arrange remaining cheese slices over lasagne, bake uncovered, further 15 minutes or until golden and cooked through. Stand 5 minutes before serving. Serve sprinkled with chopped fresh herbs if desired.
Note: Finely chop giblets and livers in food processor; do not purée.

Each pasta shape is ideally suited to a particular type of sauce. As a rule spaghetti combines beautifully with tomato, butter and cream based sauces — these rich sauces coat the long pieces of pasta well. Shorter pasta shapes like penne, rigatoni and spiral are good with meaty, chunky sauces — the meat is spread around the pasta and the sauce is trapped in and around the pasta shape. Vermicelli is ideal for creamy, cheese or egg sauces that cling to the thin pasta strands. Flat, wide pasta such as pappardelle and curly pappardelle are dressed with richly flavoured tomato and game sauces. Smaller shapes like macaroni add substance to soups and ragu's. Farfalle (bow) and conchiglie (shell) pasta are best served with other attractive ingredients like vegetable pieces, prawns or mussels. Stuffed pasta such as ravioli and tortellini are finest with subtle sauces that do not overwhelm the main seasoning. Serve light fresh tomato, simple cream or butter and herb sauces with these pasta.

Fettucine with Bacon and Red Capsicum Sauce

The bacon and red capsicum sauce is rich and creamy and is best served with fresh or dried fettucine or tagliatelle as it is a great coating sauce. Sauce freezes successfully for up to a month. When reheating, do not boil.

PREPARATION TIME: *10 minutes*
COOKING TIME: *30 minutes*
SERVES 6

½ cup dry white wine
1 spring onion, chopped
½ teaspoon whole black peppercorns
2 tablespoons butter
4 thick bacon rashers, cut into strips
2 large red capsicums, cut into thin strips
1 tablespoon wholegrain mustard
1 cup cream
500 g dried fettucine or tagliatelle
fresh parsley (optional)

1 Combine wine, spring onion and peppercorns in small pan. Boil uncovered, 5 minutes or until reduced to 2 tablespoons and remove from heat.
2 Heat butter in separate pan. Add bacon, cook over medium heat for about 10 minutes or until bacon is well browned and crisp. Add capsicum to pan, stir over low heat 2 minutes. Stir in strained reduction. Simmer covered, 8 minutes or until capsicums are soft.
3 Stir in combined mustard and cream, bring to boil. Reduce heat, simmer covered, 5 minutes.
4 Cook fettucine in large pan of boiling water until just tender, drain. Add fettucine to sauce, toss until combined. Serve sprinkled with finely chopped fresh parsley.
Note: 375 g fresh fettucine or tagliatelle can be substituted for the dry pasta in the recipe.

Left: Traditional Chicken Lasagne; Right: Fettucine with Bacon and Red Capsicum Sauce

A sprinkling of freshly ground black pepper is often all freshly sauced pasta needs.

Grated or flaked Parmesan or pecorino enhances rich tomato pasta dishes but is generally not offered with fish, seafood, game or mushroom sauced pasta.

To dress your pasta dishes never use prepared grated cheese, use only Parmesan cheese labelled *Parmigiano Reggiano* and only grate the cheese when ready to use.

The character of a flavoursome tomato sauce for pasta lies with the cooking and the cooking time. Light short simmering gives fresh, fragrant results and long slow simmering gives dark, rich full bodied flavour.

Spaghetti with Proscuitto

This strong yet delicately flavoured dish can be served with spaghetti, fettucine or tagliatelle. The sauce will coat and flavour the pasta superbly. Do not be deterred by the quantity of oil, it is simply delicious and not in the least over powering. Use good quality olive oil for this recipe.

PREPARATION TIME: *15 minutes*
COOKING TIME: *12 minutes*
SERVES 4

375 g dried spaghetti
½ cup olive oil
1 onion, finely chopped
125 g prosciutto, cut into thin strips
½ cup sliced sun dried tomatoes in oil, undrained
45 g can anchovy fillets in oil, chopped, undrained
1 tablespoon small capers, drained
2 cloves garlic, crushed
1 teaspoon dried tarragon leaves
Parmesan cheese (optional)

1 Cook spaghetti in large pan of boiling water until just tender; drain, keep warm.
2 Heat oil in pan. Add onion, cook over a medium heat for about 5 minutes or until onion is well browned then add prosciutto, cook a further 3 minutes.
3 Add tomatoes, anchovies and capers to pan, stir over medium heat 2 minutes. Add remaining ingredients, stir over low heat for 2 minutes.
4 Add pasta to sauce, toss over low heat until well coated. Serve with coarsely grated Parmesan cheese, if desired.

Chicken and Leek Tortellini

Tortellini can be frozen successfully without affecting the taste or texture of the dough and filling. Drop frozen tortellini into boiling water to cook.

PREPARATION TIME: *45 minutes plus 30 minutes standing time*

COOKING TIME: *25 minutes*
SERVES 4–6

2½ cups plain flour
4 eggs, lightly beaten
2 tablespoons water
FILLING
1 tablespoon butter
1 small leek, finely chopped
2 skinned chicken thigh fillets, chopped
2 tablespoons plain flour
¾ cup chicken stock
CREAMY ONION SAUCE
1 tablespoon butter
1 large onion, finely chopped
½ teaspoon brown sugar
½ teaspoon brown vinegar
½ teaspoon soy sauce
300 mL carton cream
¼ teaspoon cracked black peppercorns
Parmesan cheese (optional)

1 Sift flour into a bowl. Make well in centre and add eggs. Gradually incorporate into flour with a fork. Turn onto lightly floured surface and knead until smooth and elastic, about 3 minutes. Stand covered, 30 minutes.
2 Roll out quarter of the dough into rectangle about 3–mm thick using rolling pin or pasta rolling machine. Cut dough into rounds 7–cm in diameter using a plain or flutted cutter.
3 Place ½ teaspoonful of chicken and leek filling into centre of each round. Brush half the round with water, fold in half to enclose filling. Fold edges up, press corners together firmly. Repeat process with remaining dough and filling.
4 Drop tortellini into large pan of boiling water a few at a time, cook for about 3 minutes or until just tender, drain. Transfer to serving bowls or plates. Serve with creamy onion sauce, sprinkled with coarsely grated Parmesan cheese if desired.
5 To make filling: heat butter in pan. Add leek, cook over medium heat 5 minutes. Add chicken and flour, stir over medium heat 2 minutes. Add stock and stir until smooth and mixture boils and thickens. Remove from heat, cool. Process until smooth.
6 To make sauce: heat butter in pan. Add onion, stir over medium heat 10 minutes or until well browned. Add sugar, vinegar and soy sauce, stir 1 minute. Add cream, bring to boil, reduce heat, simmer uncovered 5 minutes. Stir in peppercorns.

Above: Chicken and Leek Tortellini; Below: Spaghetti with Prosciutto

For baked pasta dishes there are several cheeses which will give excellent results, the obvious choice would be mozzarella though Bel Paese and Fontina cheeses also melt in the mouth beautifully and are rich and creamy. Ricotta cheese blends well with other ingredients like spinach to give baked pasta dishes extra smoothness and flavour, to add richness and a unique flavour add a little Gorgonzola cheese to baked pasta.

Oven Baked Lasagne

A rich flavoured lasagne made with an authentic home-made Bolognaise sauce, based on beef, raw ham, vegetables and wine, complemented with a creamy ricotta and feta layer and topping. The sauce itself is traditionally served with spaghetti or tagliatelle, but is equally as good with the chunkier types of pasta such as rigatoni, spiral pasta and ravioli.

PREPARATION TIME: *30 minutes*
COOKING TIME: *1 hour 25 minutes*
SERVES 6

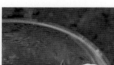

1 tablespoon olive oil
1 tablespoon butter
1 onion, finely chopped
1 stick celery, finely chopped
100 g prosciutto, finely chopped
2 tablespoons finely chopped pepperoni
sausage
500 g beef mince
½ cup dry white wine
400 g tomato purée
¾ cup beef stock
½ teaspoon dried thyme leaves
125 g ricotta cheese, sieved
100 g feta cheese, mashed
1 tablespoon chopped chives
3 eggs, lightly beaten

Oven Baked Lasagne

200 g packet pre-cooked lasagne sheets
(approximately 16 sheets)
freshly grated Parmesan cheese, to serve

1 Heat oil in butter in medium pan. Add onion and celery, cook over medium heat 3 minutes. Add prosciutto and pepperoni to pan, cook over high heat 2 minutes or until well browned. Add beef, stir over high heat 5 minutes or until beef is well browned.

2 Add wine, tomato purée, stock and thyme leaves, bring to boil, simmer uncovered, 30 minutes or until mixture is thick and almost all liquid has been absorbed. Remove from heat, cool slightly.

3 Combine ricotta, feta, chives and eggs in bowl, beat until smooth.

4 Spread a small portion of mince sauce over base of greased ovenproof dish. Top with a layer of lasagne sheets. Spoon half the remaining Bolognaise sauce over the lasagne, top with another layer of lasagne sheets. Pour half the cheese mixture over the lasagne, top with another layer of sheets. Repeat layering process with remaining ingredients, ending with cheese mixture on top. Bake lasagne on middle shelf of moderate oven for 40 minutes. Remove from oven, stand 5 minutes before serving. Sprinkle with freshly grated Parmesan to serve.

Note: Bolognaise sauce can be made and stored in the freezer for up to 1 month.

Cheesy Rigatoni with Pork Balls

The creamy, cheesy sauce is an excellent coating sauce and helps bind the ingredients together. It is a great dish that can be eaten hot or cold. The recipe can be made using medium rigatoni or large penne pasta.

PREPARATION TIME: *20 minutes plus 5 minutes standing time*
COOKING TIME: *30 minutes*
SERVES 4–6

375 g pork mince
2 tablespoons grated fresh Parmesan cheese
1 tablespoon chopped flat-leaved parsley
1 cup fresh breadcrumbs
1 teaspoon garlic, crushed
1 egg, lightly beaten
¼ cup plain flour
1 cup oil, for frying
250 g medium rigatoni pasta
½ cup halved stuffed Spanish olives
1 tablespoon finely chopped fresh mint
½ teaspoon tumeric powder
300 g carton sour cream, lightly beaten
3 eggs, lightly beaten
½ cup freshly grated Parmesan cheese
½ cup coarsely grated mozzarella cheese

1 Process pork mince, cheese, parsley, breadcrumbs, garlic and egg together until smooth. Roll two level teaspoonsful of mixture into balls; roll in seasoned flour.
2 Heat oil in small pan. Add pork balls, cook in batches until golden brown. Remove with slotted spoon; drain on absorbent paper.
3 Cook pasta in large pan of boiling water until just tender; drain.
4 Combine rigatoni, olives, mint, tumeric, sour cream, eggs and cheeses together in large bowl. Add balls, toss until well coated.
5 Spoon mixture into a well greased shallow ovenproof dish. Bake in moderate oven 20 minutes. Stand 5 minutes before serving.

Roll two level teaspoonfuls of meat mixture into balls.

Cook meatballs in oil in batches until just cooked and golden brown.

Combine rigatoni, olives, mint, tumeric, sour cream, eggs, cheese and meatballs.

Spoon mixture into a well greased shallow ovenproof dish, bake for about 20 minutes.

Spiral Pasta with Spicy Lamb

The combination of carefully selected spices, lamb, coconut cream and peanut butter in this sauce contribute to its unique rich flavour. Spicy lamb sauce is ideal served over spiral pasta, pasta bows or small penne pasta.

PREPARATION TIME: *12 minutes*
COOKING TIME: *35 minutes*
SERVES 4

2 tablespoons ghee or olive oil
2 onions cut into strips, from top to base of onion
500 g lamb leg steaks, cut into 2–cm cubes
½ teaspoon cumin powder
¼ teaspoon chilli powder
¼ teaspoon garam masala
¼ teaspoon paprika
1 tablespoon fruit chutney
½ cup coconut cream
1 tablespoon crunchy peanut butter
¾ cup chicken stock
1 clove garlic, crushed
2 small zucchinis, cut into thin rounds
1 tablespoon coriander
500 g spiral pasta

1 Heat ghee or oil in pan. Add onions and lamb, cook over high heat for approximately 3 minutes or until well browned.
2 Add spices, chutney, coconut cream, peanut butter and stock, bring to boil. Reduce heat to low and simmer covered, 20 minutes stirring occasionally.
3 Meanwhile, cook pasta in large pan of boiling water until just tender, drain.
4 Add garlic to sauce, simmer uncovered further 10 minutes. Add zucchini and coriander, stir over low heat 2 minutes or until heated through. Serve spicy lamb sauce over spiral pasta, sprinkled with extra chopped coriander if desired.
Note: If ghee is not available for this recipe, use olive oil. Do not use butter as it will not withstand the high cooking temperatures required to brown the meat and onions without it burning. The burnt flavour of the butter will be imparted throughout the sauce.

Pork Cannelloni with Mushroom Sauce

Pork and veal or chicken mince may replace the pork in this unusual version of cannelloni. The lemon mushroom sauce, tart yet slightly sweet, complements the filling beautifully. Cannelloni shells can be filled ahead of time and baked closer to serving time.

PREPARATION TIME: *20 minutes*
COOKING TIME: *50 minutes*
SERVES 4–6

2 tablespoons olive oil
500 g pork mince
125 g ricotta cheese, mashed
½ cup corn kernels, well drained
1 small zucchini, finely chopped
1 tablespoon seeded mustard
1 egg, lightly beaten
200 g packet pre-cooked cannelloni shells
2 tablespoons butter, melted
MUSHROOM SAUCE
285 g can button mushrooms, drained, sliced
1 teaspoon dried thyme leaves
1 tablespoon honey
1½ cups chicken stock
1 tablespoon cornflour
¼ cup lemon juice
1 teaspoon soy sauce

1 Heat oil in pan. Add pork, cook over high heat 5 minutes or until browned. Remove from heat, transfer to bowl, cool.
2 Combine ricotta, corn, zucchini, mustard and egg with pork, mix well. Carefully spoon mixture into cannelloni shells. Arrange filled cannelloni in single layer, side by side in greased ovenproof dish. Brush liberally with the butter, cover with foil, bake in moderate oven 30 minutes or until tender. Bake uncovered, further 10 minutes. Serve with lemon mushroom sauce.
3 To make sauce: place mushrooms, thyme, honey and stock in small pan. Blend cornflour with lemon juice and soy sauce until smooth, add to pan. Stir sauce over medium heat for about 5 minutes or until mixture boils and thickens.

Pasta is best if served *al dente*, literally meaning to the bite. It should be tender but with firmness to the bite. You may like pasta even a little harder, this is known as *fil de ferro* and can be translated as wire. Try the pasta as it is cooking by biting through a test piece, this way you can tell when the pasta is done to your likeness, you may have to test the pasta several times during cooking.

Hearty Pasta, Chicken and Vegetables

A hearty and economical family meal ideal for the colder months of the year. Serve this dish, sprinkled with coarsely grated Parmesan or pecorino cheese, with warm crusty bread to soak up the sauce.

PREPARATION TIME: *20 minutes*
COOKING TIME: *40 minutes*
SERVES 6

6 chicken wings, each cut into 3 pieces
2 tablespoons Taco seasoning mix
2 tablespoons plain flour
¼ cup oil
1 small eggplant, cut into 2–cm squares
1 green capsicum, chopped
1 onion, chopped
1 small zucchini, chopped
2 tomatoes, peeled, cut into eigths
1 teaspoon dried marjoram leaves
1 tablespoon fruit chutney
1 tablespoon lemon juice
2 cups water
125 g large shell pasta

1 Place chicken pieces in plastic bag with the seasoning mix and the flour, toss until chicken is well coated.
2 Heat oil in pan. Add chicken, cook in batches over medium heat until golden brown, drain on absorbent paper.
3 Add eggplant, capsicum and onion to pan, cook over medium heat 5 minutes stirring occasionally. Add zucchini, tomatoes, marjoram, chutney, juice and water, bring to boil. Reduce heat, simmer covered 15 minutes, stirring occasionally.
4 Add pasta and chicken to pan, stir until combined. Bring to boil, reduce heat, simmer covered, further 15 minutes or until chicken is cooked through and pasta is just tender.

Left: Hearty Pasta,
Chicken and Vegetables;
Right: Spiral Pasta with
Spicy Lamb

Pasta is best if cooked, dressed with sauce and served immediately. If this is not possible you can keep the pasta warm for a short time by draining pasta into a large colander and placing it over a small amount of boiling water. Covered, the pasta will stay hot for about 10 minutes. Toss the pasta with a little oil to prevent it sticking.

Farmhouse Rabbit Sauce with Farfalle

A richly flavoured rabbit sauce suitable in the colder months. Serve the sauce over or with bow pasta accompanied by crusty garlic bread to soak up excess sauce. The combination of wine and spices complement the rabbit superbly.

PREPARATION TIME: *5 minutes*
COOKING TIME: *1 hour 50 minutes*
SERVES 6

1 rabbit (about 800 g) cut into 8 pieces
¼ cup plain flour
¼ cup oil
1 onion, chopped
2 bay leaves
5 whole allspice
5 whole cloves
½ teaspoon ground cinnamon
½ cup beef stock
¼ cup brown vinegar
¾ cup dry red wine
1 tablespoon soy sauce
500 g farfalle (bow) pasta

1 Place rabbit pieces in bag with flour, toss until rabbit is well coated, shake off excess flour.
2 Heat oil in pan. Add rabbit, cook over medium heat for about 10 minutes or until well browned all over. Remove from pan, drain on absorbent paper. Add onion to pan, cook over medium heat for 5 minutes, return rabbit to pan.
3 Add bay leaves, spices, stock, vinegar and wine. Bring to boil, reduce heat, simmer covered, 1½ hours. Transfer rabbit pieces to chopping board. Chop flesh, discard bones. Return flesh to pan. Stir in soy sauce, stir over low heat until heated through.
4 Cook pasta in large pan of boiling water until just tender, drain. Serve rabbit sauce with pasta.

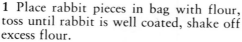

Duck Pieces served with Potato

Duck and Mushroom Sauce with Penne

You may serve the duck flavoured mushroom sauce as part of the first course with the penne pasta, and serve duck pieces as part of the second course with steamed vegetables and potatoes.

PREPARATION TIME: *10 minutes*
COOKING TIME: *1 hour*
SERVES 4–6

1.6 kg duck, cut into 8 pieces
2 tablespoons oil
1 onion, chopped
375 g button mushrooms, cut in half
2 carrots, chopped
¾ cup chicken stock
¼ cup dry white wine
bouquet garni
250 mL bottle prepared pasta sauce
250 g large penne pasta
2 tablespoons butter, melted
2 tablespoons chopped parsley

1 Place duck pieces onto grilling tray, prick skin all over with a skewer. Cook duck under grill at medium heat 10 minutes each side. Remove from grill; set aside.
2 Heat oil in pan. Add onion and mushrooms, cook over medium heat 10 minutes. Add carrots, duck pieces, chicken stock, wine, bouquet garni and sauce to pan. Bring to boil, reduce heat, simmer covered 30 minutes or until duck is tender; discard bouquet garni.
3 Cook pasta in large pan of boiling water until just tender; drain. Toss pasta with butter and parsley. Serve duck and mushroom sauce with prepared penne pasta sprinkled with fresh chopped herbs if desired.

Above: Duck and Mushroom Sauce with Penne; Below: Farmhouse Rabbit Sauce with Farfalle

Beef Ravioli with Hot Salami

There is absolutely no match with home-made ravioli. The filling comprises beef, pine nuts, parsley and ricotta cheese and is served over a hot salami and tomato flavoured sauce.

PREPARATION TIME: *45 minutes plus 30 minutes standing time*
COOKING TIME: *7 minutes*
SERVES 4–6

2½ cups plain flour
4 eggs, lightly beaten
2 tablespoons water
FILLING
375 g rump steak
1 tablespoon butter
1 tablespoon pine nuts
2 tablespoons chopped flat-leaved parsley
1 cup ricotta cheese (about 300 g), mashed

HOT SALAMI AND TOMATO SAUCE
375 mL bottle prepared pasta sauce
½ cup chopped hot salami
½ cup water
1 clove garlic, crushed
2 teaspoons chopped garlic chives

It is advisable, when using fresh pasta in a recipe as a substitute to dried pasta, to use slightly less in quantity because fresh pasta absorbs more water and swells more than the dried varieties. Cooking time of fresh pasta is also lessened.

1 To make ravioli: see Basic Pasta Dough page 56.
2 Roll out a quarter of the dough into a rectangle 2–mm thick using a rolling pin or pasta rolling machine. Roll out another quarter to a rectangle slightly larger than the first.
3 Place a teaspoonful of filling onto the first rectangle at 5–cm intervals in straight rows. Brush the dough between filling with water. Place the second sheet of dough carefully over the top. Press down between the filling to seal sheets of dough together. Cut into 4–cm squares using a floured pastry wheel or sharp knife. Repeat with remaining dough and filling. Place completed ravioli in a single layer on a lightly floured tray, cover tray loosely with a tea-towel.
4 Drop ravioli into large pan of boiling water a few at a time, cook for 4 minutes or until just tender; drain. Spoon sufficient sauce over base of serving plates. Serve ravioli over sauce. Sprinkle with extra chopped parsley before serving if desired.
5 To make filling: process steak until almost smooth. Melt butter in pan. Add beef and pine nuts, stir over high heat 2 minutes. Remove from heat, cool slightly. Stir in parsley and ricotta cheese.
6 To make sauce: heat sauce, salami and water in a small pan. Bring to boil, reduce heat, simmer uncovered, 5 minutes. Remove from heat stir in garlic and chives.

Place the second sheet of pasta dough carefully over the top of filling.

Press down between filling to seal sheets, use a floured, serrated pastry wheel to cut pasta.

Beef Ravioli with Hot Salami

Risoni Seasoned Spatchcocks

Here's an exciting and simple recipe to prepare for a special occasion using risoni, the small rice shaped pasta. Seasoned spatchcock make an ideal main course. They may also be served as an entrée.

PREPARATION TIME: *15 minutes plus 1 hour standing time*
COOKING TIME: *1 hour*
SERVES 4

¼ cup finely chopped dried apricots
1½ cups chicken stock
½ cup risoni shaped pasta
2 tablespoons chopped pecan nuts
¼ cup dry breadcrumbs
½ teaspoon grated orange rind
2 × no.5 spatchcocks, rinsed, wiped dry

ORANGE MINT GLAZE
1 tablespoon mint jelly, warmed

½ cup orange juice
2 teaspoons soy sauce

1 Soak apricots in 1 cup boiling water for 1 hour, drain.
2 Bring stock to boil, add risoni, stirring constantly for 2 minutes. Reduce heat, simmer uncovered 10 minutes or until almost all liquid is absorbed, cool.
3 Combine apricots, undrained risoni, nuts, breadcrumbs and rind together in small bowl. Spoon risoni mixture into cavity with a small skewer or cocktail stick.
4 Brush birds with glaze. Arrange on rack in oven tray, bake in moderate oven 45 minutes or until birds are golden and cooked through. Serve spatchcocks, cut in half with the seasoning. Pour over remaining glaze just before serving.
5 To make glaze: combine all ingredients in small pan, stir over low heat 5 minutes.
Note: Spatchcock are available from specialty poultry shops and may be ordered from poultry counters in large department stores. If they are not obtainable, you may substitute the spatchcock with a large chicken.

Risoni Seasoned Spatchcocks

Spaghetti with Chicken and Chick Peas

The sauce is chunky and best served with spaghetti.

PREPARATION TIME: *15 minutes*
COOKING TIME: *35 minutes*
SERVES 4–6

1 tablespoon olive oil
1 onion, chopped
3 chicken breast fillets, finely chopped
4 thick rashers bacon, rind removed, finely chopped
440 g can chick peas (garbanzos) rinsed
440 g can tomatoes, crushed
2 teaspoons tomato paste
½ teaspoon paprika
1 zucchini, cut into thin rounds
1 tablespoon chopped coriander
2 teaspoons chopped fresh mint
1 tablespoon lemon juice
500 g dried spaghetti

1 Heat oil in pan. Add onion, chicken and bacon, cook over medium heat 5 minutes or until browned. Add chick peas, tomatoes, paste and paprika, cover. Reduce heat, simmer 15 minutes. Simmer uncovered a further 5 minutes.
2 Add zucchini, herbs and lemon juice to sauce, simmer uncovered 10 minutes.
3 Cook spaghetti in large pan of boiling water until just tender, drain.
4 Serve sauce over spaghetti, sprinkled with grated Parmesan cheese if desired.

Penne Pasta with Chicken and Pimiento

Pimiento is available in cans or jars from your supermarket.

PREPARATION TIME: *15 minutes*
COOKING TIME: *15 minutes*
SERVES 4

390 g can pimiento, drained
2 teaspoons olive oil
2 cloves garlic, crushed
1 small red chilli, finely chopped
2 chicken breast fillets, thinly sliced
½ cup chicken stock
½ teaspoon sugar
1 tablespoon chopped basil
300 g penne pasta

1 Blend or process pimiento until smooth. Heat oil in pan, add garlic and chilli, cook stirring for 1 minute.
2 Add chicken, stock, sugar and pimiento to pan, bring to boil. Reduce heat, simmer uncovered until chicken is tender and sauce has thickened; stir in basil.
3 Cook penne in a large pan of boiling water until just tender, drain. Combine penne and sauce, serve immediately.

Rigatoni with Chicken and Bacon

A delightfully flavoursome and economical main course for the family.

PREPARATION TIME: *5 minutes*
COOKING TIME: *40 minutes*
SERVES 6

2 tablespoons olive oil
8 chicken thigh fillets
125 g bacon, cut into strips
2 sticks celery, chopped
1 red capsicum, chopped
4 spring onions, chopped
4 cups water
2 tablespoons soy sauce
125 g rigatoni
1 cup frozen peas, thawed
2 cloves garlic, crushed

1 Heat oil in pan. Add chicken, cook over medium heat 5 minutes until browned all over but not cooked through. Remove from pan, drain on absorbent paper.
2 Add bacon, celery and capsicum to pan, cook over medium heat 5 minutes or until vegetables are softened. Add spring onions, water and soy sauce, bring to boil, add rigatoni. Reduce heat to low, simmer in sauce, uncovered, 15 minutes. Stir in peas and garlic, cook over low heat 5 minutes or until peas and chicken are tender. Serve sprinkled with cracked black peppercorns or grated cheese.

As a general guide if pasta is to be served as a first course allow about 75 g to 100 g per person. If the pasta is served as a more substantial main course allow about 100 g to 150 g per person.

Parmesan, earned its name from the Italian town of Parma where it was first made, it can only carry the stamp of *Parmigiano Reggiano* if it has been produced in the selected region of Northern Italy. The name *Parmesan* was declared a generic term by the Italian government because of the intense conflict between towns producing the much sought after cheese.

Above: Spaghetti with Chicken and Chick Peas; Below: Rigatoni with Chicken and Bacon

CUTTING, FILLING AND SHAPING PASTA

Fresh pasta can be cut into many shapes, sizes and lengths, the most well-liked pasta being lasagne, cannelloni and the filled shapes ravioli and tortellini. Lasagna and cannelloni are easy, you simply cut them to the size required for your own baking dish. The discipline of making ravioli and tortellini is a little more difficult but with practice and patience you will perfect this skill.

To cut pappadrelle use a serrated pasta cutting wheel and cut pasta into 30–cm long and 2–cm wide strips. Use the cutter to also make farfalle (bow) pasta, cut pasta into 2–cm squares, pinch each square together in the middle to give a bow effect.

Veal and Sage Tortellini

PREPARATION TIME: *1 hour*
COOKING TIME: *about 5 minutes*
SERVES 6

Cook tortellini until just tender, serve with a simple tomato or cream sauce.

1 quantity pasta dough
FILLING
30 g butter
1 small onion, finely chopped
150 g finely minced veal
75 g finely minced pork
2 teaspoons finely chopped parsley
2 teaspoons finely chopped sage
2 tablespoons plain flour
¾ cup chicken stock

1 Roll out a quarter of the dough into a rectangle, about 3–mm thick using a rolling pin or a pasta rolling machine.
2 Cut dough into rounds using a fluted or plain 7–cm round cutter.
3 Place a level teaspoon of filling into the centre of each round.
4 Brush half the round with water, fold in half to enclose the filling.
5 Fold the edges up, press corners together firmly. Repeat procedure with remaining dough and filling.

6 To make filling: heat butter in pan, add onion, cook stirring until lightly golden. Add veal and pork, cook stirring until just cooked. Stir in parsley and sage. Add flour, stir over a medium heat for 2 minutes, add stock, stir until mixture boils and thickens.

Cool to room temperature before filling pasta.

Note: Tortellini can be frozen successfully without affecting the taste or texture of the dough and filling. Drop frozen tortellini into boiling water to cook, there is no need to thaw them first.

Cut rolled dough into 7–cm rounds using a fluted or round cutter.

Place a teaspoon of filling into the centre of each round.

Fold each round in half to enclose the filling, press edges to seal.

Fold up edges, bend tortellini around finger, press corners together.

Pumpkin Ravioli with Butter and Pecorino

A ravioli tray can also make filling the ravioli dough much easier and neater. These trays are available from specialty kitchen shops.

PREPARATION TIME: *45 minutes plus 30 minutes standing*
COOKING TIME: *6 minutes*
SERVES *4*

1 quantity pasta dough
PUMPKIN FILLING
500 g piece pumpkin
¼ cup chopped chives
pinch ground nutmeg
SAUCE
125 g butter
freshly grated pecorino cheese
chives

1 Roll out a quarter of the dough very thinly into a rectangle, using a rolling pin or pasta rolling machine. Roll out another quarter of dough to a rectangle slightly bigger than the first.
2 On the first rectangle place teaspoonfuls of pumpkin filling at 5–cm intervals in straight rows.
3 Brush the dough between filling very lightly with beaten egg.
4 Place the second sheet of dough carefully over the top. Press down between the filling to seal the sheets of dough together.
5 Use a floured crimped pastry wheel or a sharp knife to cut into squares. Repeat with remaining dough and filling. Place completed ravioli in a single layer on a lightly floured tray until ready to cook, cover tray loosely.
6 To make pumpkin filling: place pumpkin in a small baking dish. Bake in a moderate oven (180°C) for 1 hour or until tender; cool. Remove any seeds, scoop out pumpkin and mash well. Stir in chives and nutmeg.
7 To cook ravioli: drop into a large pan of boiling water. Cook until tender, about 4 minutes; drain. Transfer to serving plate.
8 To make sauce: heat butter in a pan over medium heat until lightly browned, pour over ravioli, sprinkle with pecorino cheese and chives.

Place teaspoonsful of filling at 5–cm intervals in straight rows.

Brush the dough between the filling with lightly beaten egg.

Press down between filling to seal the sheets of dough together.

Use a floured serrated pastry cutter to cut pasta into squares.

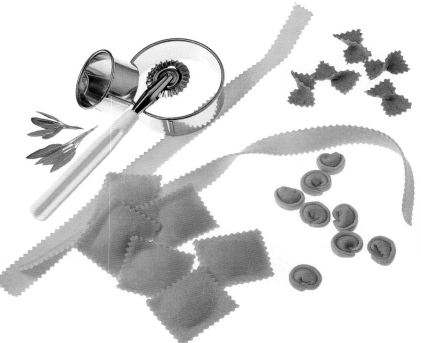

Noodles with Meat, Poultry & Game

MEAT, POULTRY AND GAME are presented with fresh and dried noodles in this assortment of recipes. We give you simple recipes that can be served as accompaniments to stir-fried dishes and hearty one-pot main course style dishes. Wheat flour noodles or egg noodles of any thickness can be used in any of the recipes using these fresh or dried noodles. Recipes that call for cellophane or rice stick noodles don't have a common substitution.

All the family will enjoy these dishes; Egg Noodle and Sticky Lamb Salad is sure to become a favourite. Included in this exceptional collection is Roast Duck Noodle Soup, Egg Noodles with Chicken and Ham, and a delicious version of Pork Chow Mein.

Above: Marinated Beef and Noodle Salad (page 103); Below: Spicy Lamb and Noodles (page 104)

Rice noodles can be found in many shapes and forms, they are most commonly sold as flat rice sticks or rice ribbons. They have varying widths and thicknesses, and are mostly sold fresh. Rice vermicelli or transparent rice noodles are thin, semi-transparent noodles, they are sold dried in small bundles. These noodles can be quickly deep-fried and will expand into crisp, white strands, ideal to use as a serving base for stir-fry dishes.

Chicken Noodle
Mushroom Soup

Chicken Noodle Mushroom Soup

Chicken is fried in a combination of sesame and vegetable oil which aids in the rich delicate flavour of this soup.

PREPARATION TIME: *15 minutes plus 15 minutes soaking time*
COOKING TIME: *15 minutes*
SERVES 4–6

2 teaspoons sesame oil
2 teaspoons vegetable oil
3 half chicken breast fillets, cut into cubes
5 cups chicken stock
2 tablespoon soy sauce
1 slice fresh root ginger
½ cup sliced dried mushrooms, soaked 15 minutes in hot water
100 g cellophane noodles, soaked in water for 15 minutes
⅓ cup snipped chives, for garnish

1 Heat oils in large pan, add chicken and cook until golden brown, remove chicken from pan, pour any remaining oil from pan.
2 Return chicken to pan add stock, soy sauce, root ginger and mushrooms bring to the boil and simmer uncovered 10 minutes. Add well drained noodles, simmer 5 minutes longer. Remove the slice of ginger.
3 Pour into large serving bowl. Garnish with chives. Serve immediately.

Roast Duck Noodle Soup

Roast duck and duck stock is the base of this tasty filling soup. Half only of the roasted duck is used, refrigerate or freeze unused portion for future use.

PREPARATION TIME: *1½ hours*
COOKING TIME: *15 minutes*
SERVES 4–6

1 tablespoon oil
1.5 kg duck, cleaned and trussed
1 clove garlic, chopped
4 spring onions, chopped
2 cups shredded Chinese cabbage
2 tablespoons soy sauce
1 tablespoon white vinegar
200 g fresh round egg noodles, cooked and drained

1 Heat oil in baking dish, add duck. Turn duck to brown all over. Pour over 1½ cups water, cover with greased aluminum foil. Bake at 180°C for 1½ hours.
2 Remove duck from baking dish and reserve stock. Cut duck into two equal portions, reserve one portion for future use. Remove meat from bone of one portion, cut into thin strips, discard any fat.
3 Add cabbage and spring onions to pan cook until cabbage softens, add soy sauce, vinegar, reserved stock and 4 cups of water. Bring to the boil, reduce heat, simmer uncovered, 10 minutes.
4 Add duck meat and noodles, simmer for 5 minutes. Serve immediately.

Oriental Noodle and Pork Soup

A delightfully quick and light soup, ideal as a starter to any meal. This soup can be made with egg or wheat noodles, if desired.

PREPARATION TIME: *10 minutes*
COOKING TIME: *15 minutes*
SERVES 6

2 tablespoons olive oil
1 teaspoon sesame oil
375 g pork fillet, shredded thinly
1 clove garlic, crushed
1 teaspoon chopped green ginger
1 large carrot cut into fine strips, 6–cm long
6 cups light chicken stock
1 teaspoon fish sauce
125 g rice noodles
1 cup small broccoli florets
3 spring onions, cut diagonally into 2–cm lengths
2 teaspoons finely chopped fresh coriander

1 Heat oils in pan. Add pork, cook over high heat for 2 minutes or until meat is browned. Remove from pan with slotted spoon; drain on absorbent paper.

2 Add garlic, ginger and carrot to pan, stir over medium heat 5 minutes. Add combined chicken stock and fish sauce, bring to boil. Add noodles, reduce heat, simmer uncovered further 3 minutes, stirring occasionally.

3 Return pork to pan with broccoli, spring onions and coriander, stir over low heat for about 3 minutes or until soup is just heated through. Serve immediately.

Note: Chinese barbecued pork can be used to replace the pork fillet in this recipe. Delete the frying step and stir the shredded pork into the soup as in step 3. The pork will impart a subtle, sweet flavour to the soup and will delicately colour the stock pink.

Left: Roast Duck Noodle Soup; Right: Oriental Noodle and Pork Soup

Egg Noodle and Sticky Lamb Salad

Lamb fillets are brushed with honey at the end of cooking time, this produces a sticky coating which firms on cooling. Lamb fillets are cooked by the Chinese roast method suspended on a rack over water. The water keeps the lamb moist and helps stop the excess marinade from burning in the baking dish.

PREPARATION TIME: *20 minutes plus 30 minutes marinating*
COOKING TIME: *25 minutes*
SERVES 4–6

¹/₃ cup soy sauce
¹/₃ cup sherry
¹/₃ cup Hoi Sin sauce
2 cloves garlic, crushed
2 teaspoons five spice powder
2 tablespoons brown sugar
2 tablespoons oil
500 g lamb fillets
2 tablespoons warmed honey
300 g egg noodles, cooked and drained
100 g snow peas, blanched
1 carrot, cut into strips and blanched
¹/₂ cup snow pea sprouts

1 Combine soy, sherry, Hoi Sin, garlic, five spice, brown sugar and oil and pour over lamb fillets. Marinate for 30 minutes.
2 Place fillets on a rack over a baking dish of water. Place in oven at 180°C for 20 minutes basting frequently with marinade. Brush with honey, cook 5 minutes longer.
3 Allow fillets to cool, cut into thin slices across the grain at an angle. Combine lamb, noodles, snow peas and carrots. Toss gently to combine.
4 Place onto large serving platter top with sprouts.

Sambal oelek is a prepared mixture of chillies, garlic, onion, sugar, salt and vinegar used in Indian cooking. The paste, is available in supermarkets, delicatessens and specialty Indian stores. Sambal oelek can be added to soups, sauces, dipping sauces and any savoury topping or filling.

Marinated Beef and Noodle Salad

This salad has a distinctive Thai flavour owing to the use of the fish sauce and sambol oelek. Purchased rare roast beef was used for this recipe, however a piece of grilled or roast beef could be used, allow to cool before slicing.

PREPARATION TIME: *20 minutes plus 2 hours marinating time*
COOKING TIME: *nil*
SERVES 4–6

400 g rare roast beef, cut into long thin strips
MARINADE
¹/₄ cup lemon juice
¹/₄ cup fish sauce
2 tablespoons soy sauce
3 teaspoons brown sugar
2 teaspoons sambol oelek
SALAD
300 g fresh wheat noodles
1 butterhead lettuce, torn into bite-sized pieces
1 cucumber, peeled, seeded and sliced
1 red onion, sliced
1 cup mint leaves, roughly chopped
1 cup coriander, roughly chopped

1 Combine marinade ingredients, pour over beef, cover and marinate for 2 hours.
2 Cook noodles in boiling water until just tender, drain. While still hot, add mint and coriander and toss to combine. Set aside.
3 Place lettuce, cucumber and onion onto large flat serving plate, top with noodles. Arrange meat slices on top and pour over remaining marinade.
Note: Thai style fish sauce is a thin, salty amber-coloured sauce produced from the fermentation of salted fish. It may be labelled as *Nam Pla*. The Vietnamese version is labelled *Njoc Mam*.

Above: Egg Noodle and Sticky Lamb Salad; Below: Egg Noodles with Chicken and Ham (page 104)

103

Egg Noodles with Chicken and Ham

Garam masala is a fragrant spice with a unique flavour comprising of black peppercorns, caraway seeds, whole cloves, cardamom seeds, fennel seeds and cinnamon bark which are dry roasted in the oven or in a non-stick fry pan until golden. They are cooled, then ground to a powder with a mortar and pestle.

Dried egg noodles are soaked in water to soften, fresh noodles may be used, they do not require soaking. The use of cooked chicken and ham makes this a quick and easy recipe to prepare, tasty and satisfying to eat.

PREPARATION TIME: 20 minutes plus 5
minutes soaking time
COOKING TIME: 5 minutes
SERVES 4–6

300 g egg noodles, soaked in water
5 minutes
oil, for deep-frying
1 tablespoon chopped ginger
2 spring onions, chopped
1/2 chicken, meat removed cut into thin
strips
100 g ham from the bone, cut into thin
strips
310 g can baby corn, drained
3/4 cup chicken stock
2 tablespoons dry sherry
1 tablespoon soy sauce

1 Drain noodles well, dry between sheets of absorbent paper. Deep-frying in oil until just crisp. Drain and place onto large serving plate. Keep warm. Remove all but 2 teaspoons of oil from pan.
2 Add ginger and spring onions to pan, cook 2 minutes. Add chicken, ham and corn. Pour in stock, sherry and soy sauce, stir to combine. Cook for 3–4 minutes or until heated through.
3 Spoon chicken and ham mixture over noodles, top with sauce. Serve.

Spicy Lamb and Noodles

A boned leg of lamb is used for this recipe, remove all fat and sinew before cutting into cubes. Garam masala is the name given to a mixture of spices used in Indian or Asian cooking.

PREPARATION TIME: 50 minutes
COOKING TIME: 20 minutes
SERVES 4–6

1/3 cup oil
2 onions, chopped
2 cloves garlic, finely chopped
1 tablespoon fresh ginger, finely chopped
1 tablespoon mild curry paste
1 teaspoon garam masala
1 teaspoon cardamom
1 boned leg of lamb, trimmed cut into
cubes
1/4 cup lemon juice
500 g tomatoes, peeled and chopped
300 g egg noodles
1/4 cup chopped mint

1 Heat oil in large heavy based pan, add onions, garlic, ginger and curry, garam masala and cardamom, cook stirring 2 minutes. Add lamb, stirring constantly until it is well coated with spice mixture, add lemon juice and tomatoes. Cover and cook over low heat for 30 minutes.
2 Cook noodles in a large quantity of boiling water until just tender. Drain.
3 Place noodles on serving plate, spoon lamb over noodles. Sprinkle with mint and serve.

Steamed Pork and Vegetables with Soy Noodles

Pork and vegetables flavoured with sherry and steamed until just cooked, be sure not to overcook otherwise the delicate flavour of the pork and crisp vegetable texture will be destroyed. Any combination of vegetables can be used.

PREPARATION TIME: 30 minutes plus 10
minutes marinating time
COOKING TIME: 10 minutes
SERVES 4–6

2 tablespoons dry sherry
500 g pork fillet, cut into thin slices
1 carrot, cut into thin slices
1 parsnip, cut into thin slices
1 stick celery, cut into thin slices

300 g thin fresh egg noodles
3 tablespoons soy sauce
1 tablespoon sweet sherry
2 teaspoons brown vinegar
½ teaspoon sesame oil
extra soy sauce, for serving

1 Pour sherry over pork and allow to marinate 10 minutes. Place vegetables into top of steamer add pork. Pour over any remaining sherry and simmer 8–10 minutes.
2 Cook noodles in large quantity of boiling water until just tender. Drain.
3 Combine soy sauce, sweet sherry, brown vinegar and sesame oil and add to noodles stirring gently to combine. Place noodles onto large serving platter and place vegetables on top. Serve accompanied by extra soy sauce.

Ginger and Garlic Noodles with Veal

Well flavoured noodles topped with tender veal strips.

PREPARATION TIME: *10 minutes*
COOKING TIME: *10 minutes*

SERVES 4–6

250 g thick egg noodles
1 tablespoon vegetable oil
1 × 5-cm piece ginger, cut into fine slivers
1 spring onion, cut into fine shreds
1 tablespoon soy sauce
1 tablespoon oyster sauce
extra 1 tablespoon oil
500 g veal steaks, cut into strips
1 onion, cut into thin wedges
1 red capsicum, cut into thin strips
2 tablespoons soy sauce
¼ cup chicken stock
1 tablespoon brown sugar

1 Cook noodles in large quantity of boiling water until just tender. Drain and set aside.
2 Heat oil in large pan or wok, add ginger, garlic and spring onion cook 2–3 minutes. Add noodles, soy and oyster sauce, toss well to combine. Place onto serving plate, keep warm.
3 Heat extra oil in pan, add veal in 4 batches cook quickly on high heat. Add onion and capsicum to pan fry 2 minutes return veal add soy, stock and brown sugar, stir to combine, cook 3 minutes.

Steamed Pork and Vegetables with Soy Noodles

Ginger is the root of the perrenial plant of the same name. Fresh ginger can be purchased from most green grocers. It is best stored in the vegetable crisper in the refrigerator to prevent it from drying out. For longer storage, peel and place into glass jar and cover with dry sherry, place the lid on the jar and refrigerate. When needed remove and slice, chop or grate the required amount.

Egg Noodle and Chicken Rolls

Fresh egg noodles have been used for this recipe. If substituting with dried noodles soak in water and pat dry before using. Rolls are placed on shredded cabbage or lettuce to prevent them from drying out and sticking to the steamer. The rolls can be served as an entrée or as part of main meal.

PREPARATION TIME: *25 minutes*
COOKING TIME: *7–8 minutes*
MAKES *8 rolls*

〉〈〉〈〉〈

200 g *thin fresh egg noodles*
8 *spinach leaves, softened for*
1 *minute in hot water*
180 g *chicken mince*
2 *teaspoons soy sauce*
2 *teaspoons sweet sherry*
6 *Chinese mushrooms, soaked and sliced*
8 *cabbage or lettuce leaves, shredded*

1 Divide noodles into 8 even bundles. Spread each bundle out to full length onto benchtop or chopping board.
2 Combine chicken mince with soy sauce and sherry. Divide into 8 equal sausage shaped portions place onto spinach, top with mushroom slices. Roll spinach leaf up to enclose filling. Wrap noodles around spinach roll.
3 Place shredded cabbage or lettuce into bamboo or metal steamer. Place rolls on top in single layer. Cook over simmering water until noodles and filling are just cooked. Serve immediately.

Divide chicken mixture into eight equal sausage shapes.

Place chicken onto spinach leaf, top with mushrooms, roll up.

Lay noodles out to full length, wrap noodles around spinach roll.

Egg Noodle and Chicken Rolls

Crispy Duck and Noodles in Five Spice Sauce

Fresh and frozen ducks are available from poultry specialty shops or supermarkets. For this recipe the duck meat has been left on the bone, if preferred, meat can be removed. The back of the duck contains little or no meat and is usually discarded, however in this recipe it is not, being deep-fried it produces a wonderful crispy skin which is delightful to eat.

PREPARATION TIME: *35 minutes*
COOKING TIME: *10 minutes*
SERVES 4–6

1.5 kg duck, washed and dried well
cornflour, for coating
oil, for deep-frying
1 teaspoon grated ginger
1 teaspoon five spice powder
½ cup sliced water chestnuts
½ cup sliced bamboo shoots
1¼ cups chicken stock
2 teaspoons soy sauce
½ teaspoon sesame oil
250 g flat egg noodles
2 teaspoons cornflour, blended with
1 tablespoon dry sherry

1 Cut duck into small pieces coat with cornflour. Heat oil in large pan or wok. Add duck pieces a few at a time cook until golden brown and cooked through. Drain and keep warm.
2 Remove all but 2 teaspoons of oil from pan add ginger and five spice powder, fry 1 minute. Add water chestnuts and bamboo shoots, cook 2 minutes. Add chicken stock, soy sauce and sesame oil bring to the boil, simmer 3 minutes.
3 Cook noodles in boiling water until just tender. Drain. Place onto large serving platter. Place duck on top.
4 Add blended cornflour to sauce, stir until mixture boils and thickens. Pour over duck and noodles. Serve immediately.

Pork Chow Mein

Pork fillet is the best cut of pork to use for stir-fry recipes as it contains no fat and is very easily cut into thin strips. Chinese dried mushrooms require 20 minutes soaking in hot water before using. Discard stalk as it is tough to serve.

PREPARATION TIME: *25 minutes plus 20 minutes soaking time*
COOKING TIME: *10 minutes*
SERVES 4–6

225 g thin fresh egg noodles
1 tablespoon oil
500 g pork fillet, cut into thin strips
1 large onion, cut into thin wedges
1 green or yellow capsicum, cut into
2-cm squares
8 large Chinese mushrooms, cut into
thin slices
2 teaspoons cornflour
2 tablespoons soy sauce
1 tablespoon oyster sauce
½ cup chicken stock
green tops of spring onions shredded, for
garnish

1 Place noodles in pan of boiling water cook until just tender. Drain well.
2 Heat oil in large pan or wok. Add pork in small batches, stir-fry each batch until cooked. Add onion and capsicum, stir-fry 2 minutes, add mushrooms fry 2 minutes longer. Stir in combined cornflour, soy, oyster sauce and stock bring to the boil, cook 1 minute. Return all pork and well drained noodles to pan or wok, toss well to combine, allow to heat through completely.
3 Place onto large serving platter. Garnish with spring onion shreds.

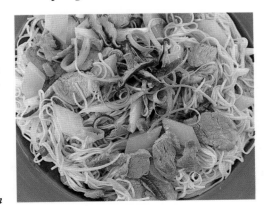

Pork Chow Mein

Spring onion curls make a simple yet attractive garnish sprinkled, just before serving, over any pasta or noodle dish. Use the green parts of the spring onions to make the curls. Cut into thin strips about 6–cm long, and place in a bowl of iced water and stand 20 minutes. The spring onions pieces will curl in at that time, drain and they are ready to be used as a garnish.

USEFUL INFORMATION

Recipes are all thoroughly tested, using standard
metric measuring cups and spoons.
All cup and spoon measurements are level.
We have used eggs with an average weight of 55 g
each in all recipes.

WEIGHTS AND MEASURES

In this book, metric measures and their imperial equivalents have been rounded out to the nearest figure that is easy to use. Different charts from different authorities vary slightly; the following are the measures we have used consistently throughout our recipes.

OVEN TEMPERATURE CHART

	°C	°F	Gas Mark
Very slow	120	250	½
Slow	150	300	1–2
Mod. slow	160	325	3
Moderate	180	350	4
Mod. hot	190	375	5–6
Hot	200	400	6–7
Very hot	230	450	8–9

LENGTHS

Metric	Imperial
5 mm	¼ in
1 cm	½ in
2 cm	¾
2.5 cm	1 in
5 cm	2 in
6 cm	2½ in
8 cm	3 in
10 cm	4 in
12 cm	5 in
15 cm	6 in
18 cm	7 in
20 cm	8 in
23 cm	9 in
25 cm	10 in
28 cm	11 in
30 cm	12 in
46 cm	18 in
50 cm	20 in
61 cm	24 in
77 cm	30 in

CUP AND SPOON MEASURES

A basic metric cup set consists of 1 cup, ½ cup, ⅓ cup and ¼ cup sizes.

The basic spoon set comprises 1 tablespoon, 1 teaspoon, ½ teaspoon and ¼ teaspoon.

1 cup	250 mL/8 fl oz
½ cup	125 mL/4 fl oz
⅓ cup (4 tablespoons)	80 mL/ 2½ fl oz
¼ cup (3 tablespoons)	60 mL/2 fl oz
1 tablespoon	20 mL
1 teaspoon	5 mL
½ teaspoon	2.5 mL
¼ teaspoon	1.25 mL

LIQUIDS

Metric	Imperial
30 mL	1 fl oz
60 mL	2 fl oz
100 mL	3½ fl oz
125 mL	4 fl oz (½ cup)
155 mL	5 fl oz
170 mL	5½ fl oz (⅔ cup)
200 mL	6½ fl oz
220 mL	7 fl oz
250 mL	8 fl oz (1 cup)
280 mL	9 fl oz
300 mL	9½ fl oz
315 mL	10 fl oz
350 mL	11 fl oz
375 mL	12 fl oz
410 mL	13 fl oz
440 mL	14 fl oz
470 mL	15 fl oz
500 mL	16 fl oz (2 cups)
600 mL	1 pt (20 fl oz)
750 mL	1 pt 5 fl oz (3 cups)
1 litre (1000 mL)	1 pt 12 fl oz (4 cups)
1.5 litres	2 pt 8 fl oz (6 cups)

DRY MEASURES

Metric	Imperial
15 g	½ oz
30 g	1 oz
45 g	1½ oz
60 g	2 oz
75 g	2½ oz
90 g	3 oz
100 g	3½ oz
125 g	4 oz
155 g	5 oz
170 g	5½ oz
200 g	6½ oz
220 g	7 oz
250 g	8 oz
280 g	9 oz
300 g	9½ oz
350 g	11 oz
375 g	12 oz
400 g	12½ oz
425 g	13½ oz
455 g	14½ oz
470 g	15 oz
500 g	1 lb (16 oz)
750 g	1 lb 8 oz
1 kg (1000 g)	2 lb
1.5 kg	3 lb

Capsicum — sweet red or green peppers
Eggplant — aubergine
Flour — use plain all purpose unless otherwise specified
Snow Peas — mangetout

THE PUBLISHER THANKS THE FOLLOWING
FOR THEIR ASSISTANCE IN THE
PHOTOGRAPHY FOR THIS BOOK:

CORSO DE' FIORI

COUNTRY TRADERS

GREGORY FORD ANTIQUES

IN MATERIAL

LIMOGES

ROYAL DOULTON

VILLEROY AND BOCH

WATERFORD WEDGEWOOD

Food Editor: Jo Anne Calabria

Home Economists: Kerry Carr, Kerrie Ray,
Voula Manzouridis

Art Direction and Design: Elaine Rushbrooke

Photography: Ray Joyce

Illustrations: Barbara Rodanska

Finished Art: Ivy Hansen

Index: Michael Wyatt

CLB 4465
This edition published in 1995 by
Colour Library Books Ltd, Godalming, Surrey
© Murdoch Books 1992
Murdoch Books is a trademark of Murdoch Magazines Pty Ltd
Printed in Singapore by Tien Wah Press
ISBN 1-85833-379-2